Fables from India

THE
PILLAR OF JUSTICE

AND
OTHER STORIES

Other Titles in the *Fables from India* Series

A Crocodile Makes History and Other Stories

The Beginning of the Mahabharata and Other Stories

The Happy Monk and Other Stories

Fables from India

THE
PILLAR OF JUSTICE

AND
OTHER STORIES

BASED ON
INDIAN AFTER DINNER STORIES BY
A.S. PANCHAPAKESA AYYAR

COMPILED AND EDITED BY
TERRY O'BRIEN

RUPA

Published by
Rupa Publications India Pvt. Ltd 2013
7/16, Ansari Road, Daryaganj
New Delhi 110002

Sales centres:
Allahabad Bengaluru Chennai
Hyderabad Jaipur Kathmandu
Kolkata Mumbai

ISBN: 978-81-291-2074-8

Second impression 2023

10 9 8 7 6 5 4 3 2

Typeset by Innovative Processors, New Delhi

Printed in India

Contents

Introduction

India is a land of myriad colours. With its rich history of folklore, India abounds in stories that have enthralled readers from time immemorial.

The oral tradition of narrating stories has ensured that these stories have been passed down from generation to generation. This exciting collection brings together a few of these classic tales for the young reader.

Common Sufferings

Dushyanta was a righteous king of the great house of Puru. He met the beautiful Sakuntala in a hermitage. Both fell in love with each other at once. He married her by gandharva rites. When they were sitting absorbed in each other and wholly oblivious of the world outside, the sage Durvasas went to the hermitage, hungry and thirsty. It was Sakuntala's duty to receive Durvasas as a guest and attend to his wants. But, in her new-born love, she did not see the sage standing at the threshold. He, too, was unwilling to intrude on the lovers and ask for hospitality. So he went away, hungry and thirsty and cursed the lovers thus:—'As Sakuntala did not recognize me in my need, so may Dushyanta not recognize her in her need! As Dushyanta has been the cause of my suffering from hunger, may he then hunger for a child!'

Dushyanta went back to Hastinapur, his capital, promising to receive Sakuntala in his court as his queen when she was formally sent there by the sage Kanva, after his return. Sakuntala was then in the family way, but neither she nor Dushyanta knew it. Dushyanta gave Sakuntala his signet ring on parting so that she might show it to him in court as a token of his pledge.

The sage Kanva came back and learnt the story of her marriage from Sakuntala. In due course, Sakuntala brought forth a glorious son, Bharata. Some months later, she and her son were escorted to Dushyanta's court by some disciples of Kanva. In washing herself in a river on the way, Sakuntala dropped her ring in the water. A fish swallowed it, and it was lost.

On reaching the court, Dushyanta did not recognize her or her child owing to the curse of Durvasas and the loss of the signet ring. Dushyanta's heart was won by Sakuntala's beauty and Bharata's charm. Still, as an Aryan king, he did not want to claim what was not his, or to graft on his glorious family tree a chance mistletoe. So he firmly refused to acknowledge them whom he had clean forgotten. Dejected and disillusioned, sad and humiliated, Sakuntala went back with Bharata to Bharadvaja's hermitage.

Dushyanta too was stricken with sorrow, and his heart ached as he had no child and had lost Bharata. When he was sitting in his hall of justice, one day, thinking over his secret grief which was gnawing at his heart, his minister came and announced that a very rich merchant had died in his dominions leaving only a pregnant wife behind and that therefore the whole property of the dead man would vest in the king. 'What about the unborn child?' asked Dushyanta. 'Sire, it cannot inherit anything, since it will have no father alive when it is born,' replied the minister. 'Am I to be always the foe of unborn children?' asked Dushyanta. 'No. Let them proclaim at once that the king is the father of all unborn children. Then shall every posthumous child have a father living when it is born and shall inherit the property.' 'Thus, every Bharata profits by his Bharata,' said the minister to his wife that night. 'Common sufferings make the whold world kin.'

Meeting in the Forest

One day, Akbar went out hunting in a forest close to Agra, the capital of his kingdom. As always, the king was accompanied by a number of men, but as he liked to ride fast, he soon got separated from the rest of his followers. Only a few men were left with him. Exhausted by the ride, the hunters suddenly realised that they had come so far that they were now completely lost. They had no idea how to get back to Agra. They rode on until they came to a place where three paths met. However, there were no road signs, and they could not decide which path to take home.

As they were discussing the matter, a young village lad came along. He stared curiously at the richly dressed hunters on their horses. Akbar summoned the boy and asked, 'Can you tell us which road goes to Agra?'

With a twinkle in his eyes, the lad smiled. 'Huzoor, how can this road go to Agra or anywhere else? Roads cannot move!'

The courtiers held their breath, shocked by the boy's impertinence. Surely the king would punish him for his rudeness. But the boy continued, 'People go from place to place. But roads cannot travel. Everyone knows that!'

Akbar was taken aback, and stared at the cheeky lad. Then he began to laugh. He always loved a good joke, even if it was at his own expense. He laughed until tears rolled down his cheeks.

'Very well, roads do not move. Can you at least find us some water to drink? We are very thirsty'

The boy willingly took Akbar and his courtiers to a well and helped them get water to drink. Akbar was quite impressed by the quick-witted, bright young lad. He looked him up and down. 'Tell me your name,' he demanded.

'First tell me yours, then I'll tell you mine,' the boy replied. Again, the courtiers were shocked by the village lad's impudence. One guard jumped up to box the boy's ears, but Akbar stopped him away laughing.

'Well, I suppose it is only fair that I should introduce myself to you after all you have done for us. I am Akbar, the Emperor of Hindustan.'

The boy bowed low, 'I am Mahesh Das, Your Majesty. I am pleased to be of service to you.'

Mahesh Das showed Akbar and his men the way out of the forest and the road to Agra. Before he galloped off, the king turned to the lad. He had been very impressed by the boy's confidence. He was poor and shabbily dressed but he was not afraid to talk with boldness and humour to rich and important men. To the king, this was a sign of courage. People such as this boy were hard to find.

Akbar took off his emerald ring and presented it to the lad. 'We need bright young men like you in the Imperial Court. Come to my palace when you grow up. This ring will help you get an appointment with me.'

Suka's Pupils

The illustrious Suka was teaching Janaka and five other Brahmin disciples in his hermitage just outside the city of Mithila. The venerable teacher used to wait for Janaka in case he came a bit late to the class; an indulgence which he never extended to the other pupils.

During his discourses on God he also used to direct his glances at Janaka most of the time and not at the other pupils. One day, the Brahmin pupils whispered among themselves, 'Our teacher talks philosophy and preaches about complete disregard for mere wealth and rank. But in practice he is like the rest. See how he addresses his discourses to him. Is it not because he is a king who can give him costly presents whereas we are only poor commoners?' Suka overheard this and wanted to show them the real reason for his discrimination.

He began a profound discourse on the nature of Brahmin and in the middle of it, caused Mithila to appear to be in flames by his extraordinary powers. Suka was saying, 'All this Universe indeed is Brahmin. From Him it preceeded, into Him it will be dissolved; in Him it breathes. Let the wise man sink his senses in his mind; his mind in reason; his reason in his individual soul; and his individual soul in Brahmin, the Universal Soul. Like the divine Ganges, Indus and Brahmaputra, that fill into the mighty ocean and lose their identity thereafter, let him merge his individual soul in the Universal Soul and lose his identity.'

The Brahmin pupils, whose attention was not riveted on the discourse, soon saw the flames at once. 'Mithila is burning! Mithila is burning!' said they to one another. 'My fine deer skin will be burnt. I must rush and save it somehow,' said one. 'And my new robes,' moaned the second. 'And my excellent conch' wailed the third. 'And my nice water jug,' shouted the fourth. 'And my stock of birch barks and palm leaves' cried the fifth. They held a hurried consultation and said to one another. 'Let us slip out and save what little we possess. Our teacher will not detect our absence because he is deeply immersed in his lecture.'

One by one, all the five Brahmins slipped out, and Janaka was left alone with Suka. Suka then told Janaka, whose whole attention was on the lecture. 'Prince, see, Mithila is burning. Your fellow pupils have gone to save their belongings. Had I not better stop in order to enable you to go and save your wealth from destruction?' Janaka smiled and said, 'Infinite is the wealth belonging to me, but none of it is in Mithila. If Mithila is burnt, Janaka loses nothing for all that Janaka values is within him and not without. So, reverend sir, proceed.' Suka too had a joyous smile on his face as he continued his lecture. He concluded it with the words: 'He is the ear of the ear, eye of the eye, tongue of the tongue, mind of the mind, soul of the soul. He is beyond sound, touch, taste, smell, form and decay, and beyond reason. Being in the midst of ignorance, and thinking in their own minds that they are intelligent and learned, the ignorant are afflicted with doubts, like the blind man's doubt of the existence of the sun, and inflict on others their own doubts, like the blind leading the blind. Take the bow of knowledge; fix the sharp arrow of unflinching faith on to it, and shoot at the immortal Brahmin, my son.' Just as he had finished, the other pupils returned with silly faces and said that they had been deceived and that Mithila was not really burning.

'Do you see now why I wait for Janaka and address my discourses to him?' asked Suka. All the five Brahmins bowed their heads in shame and remained silent.

The Dishonest Gatekeeper

After his meeting with Akbar in the forest, Mahesh Das often looked at the emerald ring the king had given him. It was a big, handsome ring with a huge sparkling emerald in the centre. It was very impressive and, no doubt, very expensive. A man with such a ring would surely be very powerful.

Mahesh Das had spent his entire young life in the village but he was now ready to travel the world. He had heard many stories about the big city and the king's palace. It sounded like an exciting place to be in and he decided to pay the king a visit and see if he could get a job at the court. Putting his few clothes and the emerald ring in a bundle, Mahesh Das took off on the road to Agra. For a simple village boy, this was truly an exciting adventure. There were many crowded bazaars along the route to the royal city.

Merchants and traders from all over the empire sold their wares here. Mahesh Das had never seen some of the things that were being sold in the markets before.

He finally arrived at the king's fort and was quite awed by its magnificence. The massive walls towered over him. He had to tilt his head all the way back to see the very top.

Outside the entrance, a man was beating on a huge drum. He announced that the king was about to hold public court. Supposedly, any of the emperor's subjects could go in and see him, but access to the king wasn't quite that simple. Tall sentries with lances and swords stood barring the way. A crowd of people waited around them. Many had come from far to bring their problem to the king's attention. Some people had pieces of paper on which their petitions were written. Others had letters from important men advancing their causes. Still others were bribing the guards to allow them to enter.

Mahesh Das pushed his way through the crowd and went up to one of the gatekeepers. 'I have come to see the king. May I go in?' he asked politely.

The tall sentry looked down in amazement at the shabby, young village boy. This young fellow was obviously entirely ignorant of the ways of the world. Anyway, he didn't look as though he had the money to offer a decent bribe. The guard began to ridicule him.

'Ah, so you've come to see the king, have you? Do you have a personal invitation from His Majesty to dine with him in his private dining chamber? Or perhaps you are so important that the emperor will leave everything he is doing to chat with you. Off with you, miserable scamp! The king doesn't have time for the likes of you.'

Mahesh Das was a bit intimidated but he held his ground. He remembered the emerald ring. Quickly he took it out of his bundle and showed it to the guard.

'The king gave me this ring some years ago. He said it would help me get an appointment with him.'

Stunned, the guard examined the ring. He showed it to the other guards. It appeared to be genuine.

The sentry wondered thoughtfully. Perhaps the young man was not as unimportant as he seemed. Perhaps he was not too poor either, and could afford to give the gatekeeper a gift. 'If I let you in, what will you give me? A cow, a hen, embroidered slippers, a silken gown... Everyone gives me something.'

'At the moment, I have nothing with me,' said the boy, thinking quickly. 'But surely the king will give me a reward and that I will gladly share with you— half mine, half yours. '

'You have to come back out this way. Mind you keep your word…or else,' the greedy gatekeeper said threateningly. He let Mahesh Das in, brandishing his sword.

The grandeur of the Public Hall of Audience took the villager's breath away. The buildings were made of red sandstone and the floors were covered with beautiful carpets. More than a hundred richly carved pillars surrounded the courtyard where the common people stood to see the king. In an enclosed balcony, on a platform covered with rich silken fabrics, sat the emperor supported by bolster cushions. He was wearing simple but costly garments. The nobles around him wore magnificent brocades. Mahesh Das was quite awed by the splendour of the palace.

When the officer of the court signalled him to approach the King, Mahesh Das stumbled forward and bowed his head as he had seen the others do. Then he held out the emerald ring, and stood silently, unable to speak. Akbar had a sharp memory and immediately recognized the ring and the boy who had helped him out of the forest.

He smiled kindly. 'So, Mahesh Das, you decided to pay me a visit after all! Tell me what would you like to have? I never rewarded you for your help in the forest. You can name your gift.'

By this time, Mahesh Das had recovered his composure. He was still smarting from the treatment he had received at the hands of the greedy guard. He bowed again and said, 'The sight of Your Majesty is reward enough for me. But if you insist on giving me something as a token of your regard, then I would like to receive one hundred lashes on my bare back.'

Akbar and all his courtiers were astounded by this peculiar

request. The boy looked poor. Akbar expected him to ask for gold or jewels but instead he asked to be beaten! This was most strange.

Akbar looked closely at the boy's face. He seemed to be suppressing a smile. This was a very intelligent young person. He was trying to tell the emperor something in his own way. He summoned the court soldier who stood by with his whip, waiting to punish whomever the emperor ordered.

'Mahesh Das, if this is what you really want I will order my man to give you a hundred lashes on your bare back.'

The soldier lifted his whip and Mahesh Das removed his shirt, but before the soldier began his task, the lad help up his hand.

'First, I must keep my promise to the sentry at the gate. I assured him that I would share whatever I received from the emperor with him—half mine, half his. Can he get his fifty lashes first?'

Akbar was furious. So this is what the corrupt guards did to the poor people who came to see their king! They demanded bribes and gifts. Akbar had the dishonest gatekeeper brought into the open court. When the man saw Mahesh Das, he realised that the boy had complained about him. He threw himself at Akbar's feet and begged for mercy. The emperor sternly ordered that all hundred lashes be given to the man as a lesson to him and to his fellow gatekeepers.

Akbar turned to Mahesh Das. He was very pleased at the way in which the clever young man had paid the dishonest gatekeeper back for his greediness. His actions confirmed what Akbar had thought at his first meeting—that Mahesh Das was an intelligent and quickwitted fellow. Even though he was poor, he had the courage to stand up to bullies and the wits to set them right.

He said to his visitor, 'I need people like you around me,

Mahesh Das. Honest and brave men are difficult to find. Stay on at court and help me run my kingdom.'

And this was the beginning of a lifelong friendship between the two men.

The Pillar of Justice

As the 'shadow of God on earth', it was the emperor's duty to establish peace and order in his kingdom by protecting the weak and punishing the wicked.

Akbar prided himself on his fairness. To his people he was 'Jahanpanah', The Refuge of the World. If he couldn't help his subjects with their problems, nobody could. Every day, Akbar and his advisors, including Birbal, sat in the Hall of Public Audience to hear people's grievances. They would spend several hours listening to reports, conducting the business of the empire and hearing cases brought before the court. A large drum would be beaten loudly to announce to the public that the king was holding court, and even common folk could then be admitted into Akbar's presence if they had any complaints or requests.

Akbar observed the accused carefully to see from his expression and behaviour if he was telling the truth. According to his biographer Abul Fazl, when Akbar judged cases, he did not rely only on the evidence presented, which could be tampered with by crafty people. Instead, he paid attention to contradictions in the narratives and the expressions of the people involved. He also took into account his own knowledge and experience.

In his judgments, the emperor was advised by the *ulama*, who were specialists in Muslim law. Strict laws were laid down to help the *qazis* (judges) in administering justice. Islamic law consisted of two parts—religious, which applied only to

Muslims, and secular, for Muslims as well as non-Muslims. (Later in his reign, Akbar made a new rule that learned Brahmins, rather than Muslim *qazis*, should decide cases involving Hindus.) Decisions would be made in consultation with the law officers, scribes would take detailed notes and the clerks would draw up the orders. Then the judgments and orders would be sent to the proper official under the imperial seal.

In 1578, when Akbar visited Punjab, he found that the legal system there was in a mess. Afghan traders, who had recently settled in the towns and villages, seemed to be taking advantage of the helpless. Birbal was sent off with another nobleman to Punjab to inquire into the matter and to help the needy obtain land from the government.

As a result of this and other such experiences, Birbal became very concerned about the oppression of the poor. In 1582 at the New Year Festival, Birbal requested that trustworthy individuals be posted at the gates of the palace to make certain that anyone who had been wronged would be able to complain directly to the king.

In 1583, Akbar established a Department of Administration and appointed his most trusted nobles, including Birbal, as overseers.

In many stories, Birbal is portrayed as the guardian of the innocent. He solves criminal cases and convicts the guilty using his common sense and knowledge of human nature. Like Akbar, he does not rely on oaths and witnesses, but observes individuals closely and catches the inconsistencies in their testimonies.

The Tree Witness

One day, an old man came weeping and wailing to the Hall of Public Audience. 'Justice, Jahanpanah! I have been robbed in my old age! Only you can help me!'

Akbar looked at the man's grey hair and wrinkled face. He was bent over and frail and leaned on a staff. His faded turban and tattered garments showed that he was quite poor. 'Tell me your troubles, babaji,' the king said kindly. 'Birbal and I will try to help you.'

'Last year, before leaving on a long pilgrimage, I had left a bag of gold coins—my entire life's savings—with my neighbour for safekeeping. When I returned, he refused to give my money back. He claimed I had never given him any money at all. I am ruined! Who will take care of me in my old age, Jahanpanah?' The poor fellow began sobbing and crying all over again. If the king could not help him, he would have to beg for a living, or starve!

'Bring your neighbour to court tomorrow morning and Birbal will help me determine the truth,' the emperor said.

Next morning, the old man came to court with his neighbour, a strong young man.

'The old baba is mistaken, Your Majesty,' said the young man, stroking his moustache. 'He is becoming forgetful in his old age. I am a rich man and an honest one. Why would I want to rob a poor old fellow, old enough to be my grandfather?'

Somehow, Birbal didn't quite trust the young neighbour. He turned to the old man. 'Did you have a witness, babaji? Did anyone see you giving the bag of gold to your neighbour?'

'No, Huzoor,' the old man said shaking his head sadly. 'I never thought I needed a witness. I trusted this young man as a son. Now I see I was mistaken.' His shoulders slumped in despair.

'Hmm…let me think,' said Birbal. 'Can you remember where you were, babaji, when you gave him this bag of coins?'

'Ah, that I do remember, Huzoor,' the old man said, brightening up. 'We were standing under a mango tree, in a mango grove outside our village. It was summer and the mangoes were ripe, and the air was filled with their delicious perfume.'

'A mango tree,' said Birbal delighted, clapping his hands. 'I thought you said you had no witness. That mango tree is your witness. Babaji, go immediately to the mango grove and ask the tree to come to court.'

A hushed laughter broke out among the nobles and other spectators. Everyone thought Birbal was joking. How could a mango tree come to court and give witness? A tree cannot walk or talk.

The old man was bewildered. But he was afraid to talk back to the king's minister, especially in front of all these richly dressed, important looking people. So he bowed low and left immediately for the mango grove.

An hour passed and the king and nobles were becoming restless. 'Be patient,' said Birbal. 'The old gentleman will be back any minute.'

'Oh no!' said the young neighbour, jumping up.'He is not going to be back for several hours. He could not even have reached there yet!'

Birbal looked at the young man. 'Tell me, how far is the

mango grove from here?'

'More than three miles away, Huzoor. But that old fellow walks so slowly, it will take him at least three hours to get there and back!'

'Very well, we shall wait,' said Birbal and proceeded with other business in the court.

Several hours later, the old man returned. He was dusty and weary and, of course, there was no tree with him. 'Thrice I repeated your order to the tree, Huzoor. But it would not budge. Now I am truly lost for I have no witness.' His face crumpled and his whole body shook with sobs.

'Don't worry, babaji,' said Birbal kindly. 'That mango tree has already borne witness for you.' He turned to the neighbour with an angry frown. 'You, young man, are a liar and a thief. You did take the old man's money under a mango tree. How else would you know which mango tree and how far away it was?'

The emperor and his courtiers burst into applause. Birbal had solved yet another case! The neighbour was ordered to give the old man not one bag of gold coins but two, and was then led away to jail. The old man went away singing the praises of Akbar and Birbal.

Whose Money Is It?

One day, as Birbal sat in court listening to cases, two men came in. One was an oil merchant and the other was a butcher. The butcher was clutching a cloth bag filled with coins. Each man claimed to be the owner of the money.

'Huzoor, I went to the butcher's shop to sell him some oil,' said the oil merchant. 'As I opened my bag to put in the coins, this greedy man was tempted by the sight of all the money and snatched my purse away. I shouted and collected people outside his shop and told them what had happened, but this rascal insists the money is his!'

Birbal turned to the butcher to hear his side of the story.

'It happened like this, Sire,' the butcher began. 'When the oil merchant came to my store to sell me oil, I left my seat next to my money box and went inside to fetch a container for the oil. When I returned, I found my bag of coins missing from the box and saw the merchant disappearing around the corner. I ran after him and caught him, but the liar insists the bag is his!'

Birbal looked from one angry face to the other. Both men appeared to be telling the truth. It was difficult to tell which one was guilty.

People in court began to whisper amongst themselves. Birbal had quite a reputation for solving complex cases. But what would he do now?

Birbal picked up the bag of money and examined it closely.

Then he sniffed it. 'Bring a vessel filled with hot water,' he ordered one of the court attendants.

When the water was brought in, Birbal poured the coins from the bag into the container. The coins sank to the bottom of the vessel, but soon drops of oil began to float upon the surface.

'Aha!' Birbal exclaimed triumphantly. 'The bag belongs to the oil merchant, since it is so oily. The butcher is the thief!'

Samudragupta and his Courtiers

The Emperor Samudragupta was playing the Veena one day. His courtiers, who wanted to flatter him, said to him, 'Your Majesty has mastered every raga and ragini to perfection.' 'You have evidently not heard the story of 'Perfection in Music,'' said the Emperor. 'Let me tell it to you to prevent such absurd flattery in the future. Narada, the supreme exponent of ragas and raginis, was once persuaded by flatterers like you to believe that he was a perfect master in them. So he went about listening to such praises everywhere, and even modestly repeated these tributes to gods and men. Sri Krishna watched this growing infatuation and wanted to put a stop to it. So he said to Narada, 'Great sage, Siva and Parvati have heard of your perfection in music and want you to give an exhibition before them.' Narada was highly elated. He set out the next day with Sri Krishna and proceeded to heaven to meet Siva and Parvati. On the way they saw a big palace where several maidens of exquisite beauty were weeping and wailing. All were mutilated in one way or other. One had an eye missing, another an ear, a third an arm, a fourth a breast, a fifth a leg, a sixth an eyebrow, a seventh an eyelash and so on. 'Oh Krishna', said Narada, his whole heart bleeding for these fair maids, 'which wretch has done this horrible mutilation?' 'Go and ask them,' said Krishna. So Narada asked them, 'What is this place, and who are you, fair sisters, and who has done this horrible thing to you?' 'Oh' said they. 'This is the palace of music, and we are the ragas and raginis. A wretch called Narada has mutilated us thus on his Veena'. Narada's pride was gone. He saw Krishna smiling. 'I shall break my Veena and play no more', said he. 'Oh, no' said Krishna 'go on playing, but realise your imperfections and try to remedy them. Don't believe idle flatterers and think you are perfect.' 'All right I have learnt a lesson. Please make my excuses to Siva and Parvati. I shall play before them when I have mastered the art a little better.' And Narada returned. And you say today that I am perfect', ended Samudragupta. The courtiers stood ashamed.

The Widow and the
Dishonest Brahmin

An old widow, who earned her living washing dishes and cleaning floors in people's homes, decided that she would go on a pilgrimage to the holy city of Benares. But there was one problem. She had saved five hundred gold coins carefully for many years so that she would not have to work in her old age, and she did not know where to leave the coins. She did not want to carry them with her, as there could be robbers and thieves on the road. At the same time, she did not want to leave them in her empty house. Her husband had died many years ago and she had no children or relatives.

She decided to go to a Brahmin who lived outside the city. He wore the orange robes of a holy man who had given up worldly matters. He sat all day meditating and praying under a banyan tree. He seemed very honest and trustworthy. She went to him and asked him to keep her money safely for her until she returned from her pilgrimage.

'O no, sister!' the holy man exclaimed. 'I have no use for worldly things like money. Please do not burden me with this responsibility. If someone steals your coins, you will blame me.'

But the old widow insisted that he help her. Finally, he agreed reluctantly. 'Very well. But you must stitch it into a bag and bury it here under the tree yourself. I will not even touch your money.'

Gladly, the widow hurried home and sewed her gold coins into a cloth bag. She then dug a hole under the banyan tree and buried her bag in it in front of the Brahmin. Thanking him profusely, she left on her journey to Benares.

'I will be back in six months and will relieve you of the responsibility,' she promised.

But six months went by and she did not return. After yet another six months had elapsed, the holy man began to think she had died on her journey. He thought about all the gold coins buried right under him. If he took all that money for himself, he could be a very rich man. After several days of thinking, he finally gave in to the temptation and dug up the bag. He unravelled the widow's stitches and took all the gold coins and replaced them with silver coins. Then he went to a tailor and had him stitch the bag back up. Pleased with himself, he hid the gold coins.

To his great dismay, almost two years after she had left, the old widow returned.

'I liked Benares so much that I could have stayed there for the rest of my life. If I had taken my money with me I would not even have come back. In fact, I may go back there once I have dug up the coins I left with you.'

Pretending that everything was fine, the Brahmin let the old woman dig up her bag and leave. She had so much faith in the Brahmin's honesty that she did not even look into the bag until a few days later. When she finally opened it, she was dreadfully shocked to find that instead of gold coins the bag now only contained silver coins of little value. She ran back to the Brahmin to complain.

'See, I knew that you would blame me if anything happened to your money. You stitched up the bag and buried it with your own hands. What do I know if your coins were gold or silver?'

shrugged the Brahmin.

The widow wept and pleaded but it did not move the dishonest man one bit. She went to her neighbours and begged them, to, help her get her money back from the Brahmin. But no one had time to help a whining old woman. She sat in her hut in despair. All she could think of was how she would have to beg for a living in her old age because she had lost all her savings. She had no one to turn to. Then she suddenly thought of Birbal. Everyone said he was the champion of the poor and oppressed.

She hurried to the king's palace and told Birbal her story. Birbal carefully examined the bag that now contained silver coins. Some of the tailor's stitches were still intact.

'Is this your handiwork?' he asked in admiration. 'This is very professional stitching.'

The old woman looked closely at the stitches and shook her head. 'Alas, my eyesight is weak, and my stitches are big and clumsy.'

'Aha!'Birbal exclaimed. 'Then that rascal Brahmin replaced the gold coins with silver ones and had the opening sewed up by a professional tailor! Is there a good tailor in your city?'

That evening, Birbal took the bag to the tailor who worked in the area where the old widow lived. The tailor remembered sewing up a bag of silver coins for the Brabmin.

Birbal returned back to the palace with the old woman. He summoned the Brahmin and publicly accused him of stealing the widow's money. When the Brahmin insisted that he was innocent, Birbal told him that he had spoken to the tailor.

The Brahmin went pale. He confessed his crime and immediately produced the gold coins and returned them to the old widow. The old lady was overjoyed to have her hard-earned savings back.

Even a King Can be Saved

King Pratapa Rudra of Orissa was a great admirer of Chaitanya. He was dying to see him and hear the words which fell from his lips and gain salvation with his guidance. He sent a messenger to Chaitanya to Puri seeking an interview. Chaitanya refused the interview, saying, 'I am a sanyasi. I have renounced everything and concentrated on God. A king is a cobra in another form. I have nothing to do with kings. I cannot see him.'

Pratapa Rudra sent the messenger back saying, 'How can you, who embraced even the brigands Jagai and Madhai, refuse to see Pratapa Rudra? Is he even more devoid of virtue than they? Is Pratapa Rudra alone to be shunned, and not saved?' 'I am sorry,' said Chaitanya, 'I cannot help it. Pratapa Rudra has many virtues, but, just as a jar of milk is shunned if it has a drop of wine in it, so too is he to be shunned despite this many virtues because he is a king.'

Pratapa Rudra was sad on hearing this constant refusal. But his desire to see the saint only increased. Dressing himself as an ordinary pilgrim he attended the car festival at Jagannath, reciting hymns and songs and verses. When Chaitanya went into a trance on hearing them, Pratapa Rudra fanned him and waited on him. On the saint's recovering consciousness, he embraced the disguised king and said, 'For all your loving attention, I can only give this embrace in return.' 'Oh, Blessed One, it is the thing I have been looking forward to all these years. I am

Pratapa Rudra,' said the king. 'I have nothing to do with kings,' answered Chaitanya. 'You have met me not as a king but as a fellow devotee. Say Govinda! Govinda!' And Pratapa Rudra and the whole assembly cried out 'Govinda! Govinda!'

The King and His People

Giving to his people was both a duty and a pleasure for Akbar. He was always looking for ways to help his subjects. He introduced an old Hindu custom into his court, where the king is weighed against valuable materials, which were then donated to the poor. Since Muslims follow the lunar calendar and Akbar used the Persian system of measuring time by the sun, he had two birthdays. On his solar birthday, Akbar would be weighed twelve times against several commodities. Including gold, silk, perfumes, copper, butter, iron, seven kinds of grain, and salt. According to the number of years he had lived, an equal number of goats, sheep and fowls were given away to people to breed. On his lunar birthday, Akbar was weighed against eight articles including silver, tin, lead, fruits, mustard oil and vegetables. This was also adopted by later Mughal emperors.

But his birthday was not the only time the king gave away donations. Every day, his clerks read out names of soldiers and guards who had never received a gift from the king, and Akbar donated horses to each person. Needy persons were supported with regular allowances. Stipends or grants of land were given to scholars, spiritual recluses and men of good birth who were unable to provide for themselves. He established eateries for the poor. Gold and silver meant for charity was kept available in the public audience hall, and several bags of a thousand coins each were kept ready inside the palace as well.

Akbar also encouraged his nobles and courtiers to be generous and to donate a certain portion of their earnings to the poor. In 1578 in Fatehpur, he had a large tank, which was about twenty yards long and three yards deep, emptied of water and filled with millions of coins, which he vowed to give away to holy men, scholars and the needy. The money was spent over three years.

Akbar liked to see for himself how people lived and whether or not they were happy in his kingdom. He did not want to rely on his officials for reports. He would disguise himself as an ordinary man and go into the streets of the city on his own. Thus he was able to observe people going about their everyday business without knowing that they were being watched by their emperor.

Akbar and the Cow

The Emperor Akbar was one day so impressed with his own power and glory that he asked his courtiers whether there was anything which he could not do. The court-wit Birbal said, 'Sire, you cannot give all that a baby needs.' 'What?' asked Akbar in anger, 'can't I even satisfy a child's cravings, I, the ruler of all this empire?' 'I stick to my words, O king', said Birbal. 'If Your Majesty wants, we can have a trial tomorrow. I shall impersonate a baby.' 'So be it,' said Akbar.

The next day, every requisite of babies was made ready at the emperor's orders. Huge cans of milk, and tins and tins of all kinds of sweetmeats and eatables were held in readiness. At the appointed hour, Birbal was put in a cradle and brought before the emperor.

'What, do you want?' asked the emperor.

'I want some freshly drawn cow's milk,' said Birbal.

'Is that all?' said Akbar, relieved very much. He got an excellent cow and had a large pail in no time.

'What do you want now?' Akbar asked of Birbal.

'Oh, put the milk back again into the udder,' said Birbal, crying like a child. Akbar stood dumbfounded and conceded his defeat by his silence.

The Emperor's Disguise

Birbal did not approve of Akbar's habit of wandering about the streets of the city in disguise. 'A king is an important man. His life should be protected. Think of what would happen to your subjects if someone were to murder you on the street. The country would be in chaos. You have a responsibility to your people to look after yourself, Your Majesty,' he protested.

'Yes, Birbal,' agreed the emperor. 'But I also have a responsibility to look after my people. 1 cannot trust the reports of the officials. You know how corrupt some of them are. I have to see things with my own eyes. Besides, it's fun!'

Akbar donned a fake beard and the faded clothes of a poor traveller. He slipped out of the palace while Birbal looked on disapprovingly.

The disguised king wandered around in the city bazaar. Pretending to be a traveller from a distant place, he asked the shopkeepers and other people he met questions about the state of affairs in the country

By and by, he realised that someone was following him. From the corner of his eye, he could see a man with a long black beard and orange garments. He wore holy beads around his neck and carried a begging bowl. He seemed to be wandering around aimlessly, but every time Akbar walked to a different shop, the holy man appeared in the background. Akbar tried to lose him by walking faster, but when he turned around, the holy man was still there. He must have walked just as fast.

Finally, Akbar decided to confront him. He stopped abruptly and walked up to the man. 'Who are you and what is your name?'

The man smirked and stroked his beard. 'My name is Wanderer.'

'What do you do?'

'I wander.'

'Where do you live?'

'Everywhere.'

The emperor began to lose patience with these cheeky answers. The man showed no respect. Akbar wanted to shake him out of his nonchalant attitude. 'Do you know who I am?'

The man smiled impudently. 'A human being just like me.'

For some reason, Akbar wanted to impress this man with his importance. 'I am the Emperor of Hindustan!'

'Oh, really?!' The man bowed in mock humility. Then he threw back his head and laughed. 'And I am the Emperor of the Universe! Now you bow to me.'

Akbar was determined to get some respect from this insolent rascal. He took his seal out from his cummerbund and held it out to the man. 'See with your own eyes. This is the royal seal. I use it to stamp all important documents. I really am the emperor.'

The man hesitated but still looked sceptical. He reached out and took the seal to examine it more closely. He held it close to his eyes. Then suddenly, he turned around and ran away before the surprised Akbar could stop him. He fled through the crowded bazaar, taking the royal seal with him.

'Stop! Thief! Catch that man!' Akbar ran after the saffron-robed scoundrel. By and by, a couple of strong men grabbed the thief.

'Let me go!' the thief commanded in an imperious voice.

'Can't you see I am the emperor?'

When his captors laughed at him, he held out the royal seal in his palm. 'See, I can prove it. This is the royal seal. Sometimes I wander about the city in disguise to see how my people are doing. Now off with all of you. Go back to your business.'

'A million pardons, Your Majesty!' Mumbling and bowing low, the people dispersed and the thief walked off.

Akbar watched all this from a hidden corner. Not having the seal to prove his identity, he was afraid to come out and challenge the thief. Ashamed of his carelessness in losing the royal seal, he walked back to the palace and slipped into his bedchamber.

Only Birbal could help him recover the seal, but he was embarrassed to tell him what had happened. After all, he had gone into the city against Birbal's advice. To his great surprise, he saw the royal seal lying by his bed, on top of a letter.

The letter was from Birbal: 'Your Majesty, now do you understand how dangerous it is for you to be wandering about the streets of the city without guards? This time you only lost your seal. Next time it could be your life.'

The relieved Emperor laughed out loud. So that had been Birbal dressed as a beggar! No doubt, he had been trying to teach his king a lesson.

The King's Parrot

The celebrated Tansen was the court musician of Akbar. The emperor was so pleased with his music that one day he said to him, 'Nobody on earth can excel you in music.' Tansen replied, 'Even within Your Majesty's dominions there are many who excel me, for instance, my own master Haridas Swami who is now at Brindaban.' 'I want to hear him before I will believe it. I am very eager to hear him,' said Akbar. 'He will not sing for any king on earth,' said Tansen; 'so, if your Majesty wants to hear him, you must come incognito.'

Akbar dressed himself as Tansen's attendant. Both of them went to Haridas Swami. Tansen saluted his master and requested him to sing a favourite song of his. Haridas refused, adding 'I don't feel like singing today.' Then Tansen adopted a clever device. He sang the song purposely wrongly. The fire in the teacher flared up. 'What!' asked he. 'Have you, in that wretched court, forgotten to sing even your favourite song properly? Hear it and realise your fall,' and he sang it correctly. So sweet and overpowering were his accents that Akbar was overpowered and saluted him and got his blessings. Then Tansen and he left. Akbar asked Tansen, 'Why is it that you don't' sing like that?' 'Because,' said Tansen, 'I am the king's parrot and have to sing whenever my king wants, whereas he is his own master and sings only when the spirit moves him.'

The Golden Touch

A soldier who had once served in the royal army died. His wife and widowed mother had no one to support them. Over the years, their savings dwindled and very little was left for the two women to live on. A neighbour suggested that they go to Birbal for advice. He was always willing to help the needy.

Birbal listened to their problems patiently. He told the old lady to appeal to the emperor for support. As Akbar was known for his generosity, he would certainly help them. But the old lady was too proud to ask for charity, even from the king.

'Very well, then,' said Birbal. 'Give His Majesty a gift. Something that has sentimental value, even if it is not expensive. If he is pleased, he will give you a gift in return. This is not begging. It will be an exchange of gifts.'

This idea pleased the old widow. The next day, she proceeded to Akbar's palace with her daughter-in-law. They were both dressed in their finest clothes. They did not wish to appear shabby and poor at this important occasion.

Birbal introduced the two women to the King. The old lady presented the heavy gift they had carried all the way from home. It was her son's sword.

'For twenty years, he fought in your army with this sword, Jahanpanah. Many an enemy did he kill with it. He was a loyal soldier and I want you to keep this as a token of his loyalty to you.'

Akbar took the weapon and examined it closely. It was old

and rusty, and not of very good workmanship. It was of no use to him whatsoever, but since the soldier's old mother had presented it to him with so much love, he could not refuse it. He gave the sword to an attendant for safekeeping and asked the keeper of the treasury to give the two women five gold coins each. He could not send them back empty-handed, even though they were well dressed and appeared to be in no need for money.

Birbal was dismayed when he heard the small amount the emperor had decided to give as a gift. He said, he would like to examine the sword, Your Majesty.'

Birbal took the sword and looked at it closely. Then he turned it over and brought it up to his eyes, staring at every inch of the weapon. He did this several times, in silence, frowning as though puzzled. Akbar was surprised by his behaviour.

'Is something wrong, Birbal?'

'Oh, nothing is wrong, Your Majesty. I just thought… Let it be.'

'Speak what is on your mind, Birbal. You seem confused.'

Birbal shrugged. 'It's just that I was so sure the sword would have turned into gold.'

'The sword turning into gold…what are you talking about?'

'Well, Your Majesty, as you know, the alchemist's stone turns all it touches into gold. I was convinced that anything which was touched by your generous and benevolent hands would turn into gold.'

Akbar understood what Birbal was hinting at. He turned to the treasurer. 'Weigh this sword and give its weight in gold coins to the soldier's mother and his wife.'

Birbal smiled in satisfaction. The two women gratefully received their gift from the king and left the palace, a million blessings in their hearts for their wise and diplomatic benefactor, Birbal.

Maya

Vishnuvardhana, the king of the Hoysalas, was a Vaishnavite and was greatly incensed at the doctrine taught by Sankaracharya, that everything here below is an illusion. He wanted to teach the exponent of this doctrine a lesson. So he invited the then Sankaracharya of Sringeri to his palace. That holy man went there and stoutly maintained that everything in this world was an illusion.

The king had previously arranged to let loose an infuriated elephant against Sankaracharya. The beast rushed at Sankaracharya who took to instant flight to save himself.

'O Venerable Sir,' shouted the king, 'why do you run so fast, seeing that the elephant is only an illusion?'

'O King,' said Sankaracharya in the course of his flight, 'my running too is an illusion. Everything in this world is an illusion.'

The Palms of Their Hands

One day, Akbar was in one of his thoughtful moods. This happened from time to time. The king liked to wonder about things: why is the sky so high, why can't deaf children talk, and so on.

Today he wondered out aloud, 'Birbal, why is it that no hair grows on my palms? I have hair on my arms, chest, face, everywhere—but none on the palm of my hands!'

As usual, the quick-witted Birbal had a ready answer. 'Your Majesty, you are always giving things away. Why, you sit here hour after hour and pass out coins to the poor and needy, as well as gifts to your officers and nobles. You are so generous, the palms of your hands are always in use; that is why no hair grows on them.'

Akbar was pleased with the answer but it did not satisfy him completely. He thought for a moment.

'Then why is it that no hair grows on your palms, Birbal?'

Birbal spread out his palms before the emperor. 'Jahanpanah, these worthless palms are always receiving gifts from you. This is why they do not have time to grow hair.'

Entertained by this line of reasoning, the Emperor had one more question. He looked around at the other nobles.

'They why is it, Birbal, that none of these men have hair on their palms either? My treasury would be empty if I was as generous as you say.'

The other courtiers waited expectantly to see how Birbal would reply.

'Your Majesty those who do not receive from you stand around wringing their hands in jealousy when they watch the good fortune of those of us who do. This is why no hair grows on their palms either.'

Akbar and everyone else burst out laughing. It was a ridiculous set of answers to an equally absurd set of questions.

The King and the Sculptor

A mighty king of Kalinga constructed the great temple of Jagannath at the cost of many lakhs of rupees. After he finished it, he advertised for a sacred sculptor who would carve an idol worthy of the temple. The reward for doing so was put at one lakh of rupees, and the punishment for failing in the enterprise was death. None offered himself for a long time. At last, one day an old sculptor came and offered to do it on one condition.

'What is that?' asked the king.

'Nobody except I should go into the temple for thirty days under any pretext whatsoever. If this condition is kept, I shall make an idol which will look just like the real Jagannath, the Lord of the Universe.'

The king was delighted. 'What an easy condition!' he said. 'I agree to it readily'. Then the sculptor shut himself up in the temple for a month with provisions, etc., and closed the massive gates. Day after day, the king and the citizens heard a thundering noise within the temple. 'Why should he make so much noise?' asked the king of his courtiers on the tenth day. 'After all, he is making but one idol. Such a noise was not heard even when the whole temple was being constructed, and there were five thousand men working then, not one.'

'It is strange,' replied the courtiers. 'Shall we go in and see?'

'No,' said the king. 'For thirty days I have promised that none should enter the temple.'

But the noise became louder and louder day by day. The king became more and more anxious as to what was happening. On the twentieth day, he again asked the courtiers:

'Whatever can this be? This noise is becoming quite inexplicable.'

'Perhaps the old fellow is breaking all the stone pillars,' suggested one courtier.

'What!' replied the king. 'Has the devil come to destroy my good temple? What shall we do? I have promised not to enter the temple for the thirty days.'

'Sire,' said one courtier, 'let us go to the temple doors and call him out. There is no harm in that. We can then ascertain from him what all this noise means.'

'Excellent,' said the king. 'Let us go at once.'

So they all went to the temple doors and called out for the sculptor. No answer came. The dreadful noise continued. The king asked his drummers and trumpeters to play their instruments. Still, no answer; the noise inside only grew the louder. 'Let us enter,' said a minister.

'No,' said the king. 'For thirty days I have promised not to enter the temple. If I do, the glorious image promised to me may be lost.'

So the party returned to the palace. That night, the noise became even more thundering, and continued right through the night. Early in the morning, the king called his ministers and courtiers and asked, 'Whatever is this? Till now, the noise was heard only during the day, now it is heard during nights as well.'

'Sire,' replied a minister, 'it looks as if the whole city will fall down soon. Why should we not go at once and break in?'

'If we do,' said the king, 'the glorious image promised may be lost.'

'But, sire,' replied the minister, 'If we do not, our glorious temple may be blown to atoms by this wretch. Even if we don't get the promised image, let us at least retain our realised temple.' The king's fears were thoroughly aroused. 'True,' he said, 'perhaps the wretch is breaking everything in our temple. Otherwise, I can't see why he should make so much noise in making one idol. Besides, the noise is heard at nights. How can he work at night without a light?'

'No light is required, sire, for breaking pillars,' said the minister.

'Ah,' said the king, 'that is the secret of the whole thing. Come, let us break the doors and enter. Even if the doors are damaged, let us save what we can of the rest of the temple.' Saying this, all went to the temple doors which were bolted from the inside. The king had them forced open, and entered the temple with his ministers and courtiers. He saw the old sculptor stooping near a misshapen idol defective in limbs and ugly to look at.

'Wretch,' said the king, 'is this the idol of Jagannath, Lord of the Universe, which you promised? You shall be beheaded for this.'

'Sire,' said the sculptor with a smile, 'your condition is not fulfilled. This is only the twenty-first day. O presumptuous king, could you not have held your soul in patience, even for thirty days, in order to see the real form of the Lord of the Universe?'

The king felt ashamed of his conduct. Nothing in the temple had been interfered with by the sculptor. He looked at the miserable idol and said, 'What can we do with this now?'

'Put it in the temple and worship it,' said the sculptor. 'The Lord resides in the ugly as much as He does in the beautiful, and in the defective-limbed as in the well-limbed. His worshippers will realise this from this idol.' Saying this, the sculptor, who was none else than the Lord of the Universe, disappeared.

The Obedient Husbands

One day, Akbar and Birbal were wandering through the streets of Agra disguised as ordinary men. Suddenly, as they were walking past a house, they heard a woman shouting and raging from within. They could not help hearing the angry words she was yelling.

'She must be screaming at one of her children,' said Akbar. 'Obviously, someone has made her furious.'

The next moment, the door of the house flew open and a man came stumbling out as though he had been pushed. His turban was thrown out after him by a woman's hand: '…and don't come back home until you get it right, you stupid man!' the same angry female voice continued. Then the door slammed shut. The man picked up his turban, dusted it off, placed it upon his head and walked away. He looked very dejected.

Birbal smiled. 'It wasn't her children she was yelling at, Your Majesty. It was her husband. It looks as though he is in a lot of trouble with his wife.'

The emperor was absolutely shocked. He could not believe that a man in his kingdom would allow his wife to treat him in such a manner. Surely his male subjects could not be that feeble!

'This man must be an exceptional coward. No other red-blooded, able-bodied man would allow his wife to speak to him so rudely,' he said.

Birbal coughed politely, the way he did when he was about to disagree with his king. 'A thousand pardons, Your Majesty, for not being able to agree with you. You are the Emperor of India—a powerful king. Men and women alike obey you and do your bidding. I cannot imagine any of your wives speaking to you in a raised voice…but for us ordinary men; it is quite a different matter.'

Akbar could not believe his ears. 'Are you telling me that this is not an exceptional case? Are you trying to tell me that most men in my kingdom are bullied by their wives?!'

'Not bullied, Your Majesty. But there is no question that our wives have a good deal of power and authority over us. We husbands know that if we want a good meal and peace in our homes, we had better listen to our wives.'

Akbar and Birbal continued to argue over the issue for several days. The emperor refused to believe that strong, capable men would allow their wives to order them around.

Finally, Birbal offered to put the matter to rest by conducting a poll. He invited all the married men in Agra to assemble in the palace yard. Hundreds of men collected there, wondering why they had been summoned.

Birbal stood up and addressed them. 'His Majesty would like to know how many of you good men obey your wives. Those who do, move to the left. Those who do not, move to the right.'

To Akbar's amazement, the entire crowd of men shuffled off to the left. So Birbal was right. All the married men in Agra obeyed their wives. All accept one. One man stood alone, away from the crowd, on the right. Akbar was delighted to see that at least one man was brave enough to stand up to his woman.

'Birbal, bring that man to me. He is a hero. I must reward him for his courage. Apparently, all the other men in my kingdom are spineless cowards,' said the emperor.

Birbal brought the lone man to the king. 'His Majesty would like to know why, when all the other men moved to the left, you remained alone on the right.'

The young man hung his head, 'My wife has always told me to stay away from crowds, Huzoor. So when all the men huddled together in one part of the yard, I moved to the other side.'

Birbal looked triumphantly at the emperor. This was, after all, yet another obedient husband. Akbar groaned.

The King and the Actor

A certain king of Travancore was once told by his minister that a very good actor had come to his city.

'What part does he act?' asked the king.

'The part of Ravana,' replied the minister, 'He plays it most excellently. By his bearing, one can realise how the real Ravana must have acted.'

'I see,' said the king. 'What is the play?'

'The embassy of Rama through Hanuman to Ravana,' replied the minister. 'Let him give a performance at the palace,' said the king. So a performance was arranged. The actor wanted to show the best that was in him. Seated on his mighty stage throne, he was hurling defiance at Rama whose prowess Hanuman was extolling. Just as he uttered the sentence, 'There is no king on earth to whom I will ever offer a seat, much less rise and bow; all, all are my vassals.' The King of Travancore went in with his ministers and generals to take his seat among the audience. The actor who was playing the part of Ravana rose and bowed to the monarch.

'Pooh!' said the king to his minister. 'Is this the actor you praised so much? The man who represents Ravana, who defied even the mightiest of kings, rises and bows down to a prince like me!' and he walked out in disgust.

Matters of Faith

Since childhood, Akbar had been very interested in spirituality and religion. When he was twenty years old, he visited the Chishti shrine of Sufi saints at Ajmer. Contact with the Sufi order had a powerful effect on the young emperor. He became very conscious of the sufferings of humanity. He abolished some laws and taxes that he felt were not humane and against the principles of Islam.

Akbar also began to visit Shaikh Salim Chishti, another widely respected Sufi who lived in a village called Sikri near Agra. Akbar was worried because he was by now over twenty-five years old and had several wives, but no male heir. Shaikh Salim predicted that the emperor would soon have three sons, a prediction which did indeed come true. In honour of Shaikh Salim, Akbar built a new capital city at Sikri along with a huge mosque, which soon became an important place of pilgrimage. Akbar named his new city Fatehpur Sikri, the City of Victory.

Akbar was interested in other religions besides Islam. He began to invite representatives from other religions to the debates at Fatehpur Sikri and at his palace. Zoroastrians, Hindus, Jains and Christians, all took part in the intense debates. Undoubtedly, Birbal would have participated in these discussions. He was probably responsible for introducing Hindu scholars and holy men to the emperor. He also taught the king a great deal about Hinduism, including some rituals that Akbar decided to follow. Akbar also showed great reverence towards the pictures of the

Virgin Mary brought for him by the European Christian priests visiting his court. He donated land to the Christians to build a church and also gave the leaders of the Sikh religion land where they founded Amritsar, their holy city

In 1582, Akbar started a new code of religious behaviour, which has come to be known today as Din illahi. It combined elements from various religions, which Akbar felt were the most important. Birbal was the only Hindu courtier to become Akbar's advisor.

The Minister and the Peon

One day, a king of Travancore overheard his peon mutter to himself. 'This is an unjust age. I, who work all day long, am paid seven rupees per month, whereas the minister, who rolls about in motor cars and idles the whole time long, is paid two thousand rupees. What injustice!'

The king wanted to show the peon the unreasonableness of his remarks. Just then, he saw a palanquin in the distance and asked the peon to go and inquire who was travelling in it. The peon went running and came back saying 'It is Sankaracharya.' 'Of which *mutt?*' asked the king. The peon went running again and came back panting and said, 'Of Sringeri *mutt.*' 'Where is His Holiness coming from?' asked the king. Again the peon ran and came back to say 'From Shencottah.' 'Where does he go to?' asked the king. The peon took another trip and on coming back said, 'His Holiness is going to Kaladi.' 'Is His Holiness going to stop here?' asked the king. Again the peon ran and when he came back he said, 'Yes.' 'For how long?' asked the king. The peon had another exhausting run and came back tired saying, 'For a day.' 'Where does he intend to stop?' asked the king. The exhausted peon ran again to the palanquin, which was going further and further, and came back and said, 'In the *mutt* attached to the temple.' 'Will His Holiness be able to see me?' asked the king. The peon had an even more exhausting journey and when he came back he said, 'Yes.' 'When?' asked the kng. Again, the peon dragged his weary body to the palanquin, which was now nearing the *mutt,* and came back and said, 'At 3 p.m.,' falling down in a heap, utterly exhausted, in the presence of the king.

The king then sent for his minister, who had not witnessed any of the above incidents, and asked him to go and enquire who had come in a palanquin that morning. The minister returned in half an hour, and, in the presence of the peon, told the king, 'Sire, it is the Sankaracharya of Sringeri *mutt.* His Holiness came from Shencottah and is going to Kaladi. He will be stopping at the local *mutt* for a day and will be able to see Your Highness at 3 p.m. today. If possible, His Holiness will also conduct the service at the temple this evening.' 'You see,' said the king turning to the peon, 'What took you nine weary journeys and five hours has taken the minister only half an hour and one single journey. Now you see the reason why you are paid only seven rupees and he two thousand rupees.' The peon stood, confounded with shame.

The Holy Man

Akbar liked everything to look perfect. 'The palace gardens and the public halls should always be neat and clean so that they make a good impression on visitors,' he said.

One day, as he was walking around the palace inspecting his land with pride, he saw a man taking a nap right in the middle of the garden under the shade of a tree. His ragged clothes were saffron, the colour worn by holy Hindu men. His beard and moustache were so shaggy that you could barely see his face. Akbar was irritated. This was no place for an unsightly beggar to rest! He went up to the man and ordered him to leave.

The man awoke from his sleep and stretched. Unconcerned by Akbar's air of authority, he asked, 'Why should I leave? Does the shade of this tree belong to you?'

'Of course it belongs to me!' said the infuriated emperor. 'So does the tree itself, the garden, the palace and everything in it, too.'

'How about the river—is that yours too?'

'Yes, this river and all the rivers in the kingdom belong to me. In fact, the whole of India belongs to me! I am the emperor.'

The saffron-clad intruder pondered this for a while. He was still not impressed by Akbar's importance. 'And before you were born, who did all of this belong to?'

'My father, of course'

'And before him?'

Akbar began to understand what the man was getting at. He dropped his arrogant attitude and sat down on the grass next to the holy man.

'The kingdom belonged to my grandfather before my father.'

The holy man said: 'So, like them, you will possess all these beautiful things during your life and afterwards they will pass on to your son and then to his son?'

'That is true,' agreed the emperor, now deep in thought. 'These possessions are mine only temporarily. I own them only while I am on this earth. Then they pass on to someone else.'

'Exactly!' said the holy man with a wise smile. 'All material things are temporary. No one really owns the shade of a tree or a rest house.'

Akbar, who was quite fond of musing about the meaning of life, said thoughtfully, 'The whole world is like a rest-house. We all stay here for a while and then move on. Is that what you are trying to tell me?'

'You are correct, Your Majesty! Being arrogant about one's material possessions is false pride.' Akbar looked up, startled at the change in the holy man's tone. He recognized the familiar voice.

'Birbal! I should have known it was you. Always provoking me to think further and deeper, aren't you!' The holy man stood up laughing and peeled off his shaggy false beard. He made a deep bow to the smiling emperor.

'It was my privilege and duty King of the World, to remind you of the true meaning of life. Vanity and arrogance are not becoming of a great mind like yours.'

Sassa's Request

Sassa, son of Dahir, was a clever Brahmin. The King of Bengal in his days was a spendthrift, neglecting his people and their affairs altogether and always playing dice and giving recurring and non-recurring grants to worthless courtiers and favourites. He had even forgotten the art of war. To stop this three-fold catastrophe, Sassa invented the fascinating game of chess. The king was delighted with it and gave up dice and played the new game for days on end, and recovered his lost interest in intellectual things and gained some valuable hints about ruling the kindom, as well as realizing how necessary the co-operation of his subjects was to a king.

So he decided to give a big reward to Sassa. Calling him, he said, 'Ask for any reward you like. You shall have it.' 'Well,' said Sassa 'give me a grain of rice for the first square on my chessboard, two for the next, four for the third, sixteen for the fourth, two hundred and fifty-six for the fifth and so on up to the sixty-fourth square, each succeeding square getting the square or the preceding. 'Is that all?' asked the king, 'How trifling a gift!' 'That is all I want,' said Sassa. The king asked his prime minister to give the number of grains demanded. After four days' continuous calculation, the prime minister came and said 'Your Majesty, there is not enough grain in all the kingdom to meet this demand, nor enough money in all the country to buy it elsewhere. It will make a mass of grain greater than the

entire Himalaya mountains and will cost millions of rupees.'
The king was astounded and incredulous, but was soon shown
the numerous calculation sheets and convinced of the truth of
the minister's statement. 'What shall I do now?' he asked Sassa.
'Sire,' said Sassa. 'I give up my demand, which was only meant
to show Your Majesty how the seemingly simple demands of
your courtiers and flatterers can ruin you kingdom.'

The king was highly pleased. He drove out the flatterers and
courtiers, cancelled the recurring and non-recurring grants to
them, made Sassa a minister, and ruled Bengal thereafter, ably,
efficiently and economically.

The Holy Name of Rama

Akbar had made it his business to learn all about the Hindus and their holy books. He even had the Ramayana, the story of Rama translated and read to him. He knew so much, he was beginning to feel all–powerful.

One day, he called Birbal and said, 'Birbal, you Hindus write the name of Rama at the top of all your writings. I am going to pass an order today, that from now on, they should write my name instead of Rama.'

Birbal pondered the matter. 'It is indeed a wonderful idea, Your Majesty, but remember one thing. When the name of Rama is uttered, even stones will float on water. So much power and magic does that word have. Are you sure that stones will float on water when your name is mentioned?'

Akbar decided to drop the idea. He did not want to appear weaker than Rama.

In the Durbar

Rulers were usually surrounded by professional flatterers—bards and poets—who would constantly remind the king of his greatness and sing his praises. The court poets were usually learned men, who were well-versed in the technicalities of poetry, grammar and literature. They also knew a great deal about politics, warfare and history, and were practised in the art of polished and ornate expression. Kings would handsomely reward the poets who pleased them the most.

Since most people could not read and write, their only way of learning about the present and past happenings in the kingdom was through the songs of bards and storytellers. Bards were known as *bhats* in northern India. Like newspaper and television reporters today, they told the common man what the king was doing. Thus, the ruler's reputation, to a great extent, depended on what the bards were saying about him.

As a result, kings usually treated the bards with great respect. Bards were usually well educated, especially skilled in the arts of music and poetry.

Another group of people who got a lot of importance at Akbar's court were artists. Art was extremely important to Akbar and his ancestors from Central Asia and Persia. Akbar had famous artists set up painting workshops for his court, which could include up to a hundred painters of different nationalities. He had many books—story books, religious works and histories—illustrated by these men. Often, several people worked on a single painting, each specialising in a certain skill. Akbar was particularly interested in portraits, especially those that were true to life; he ordered portraits to be made of all the important nobles at his court, including Birbal.

In keeping with the traditions of his ancestors, Akbar greatly valued knowledge, learning and good books. Books were precious commodities as they had to be copied by hand. Akbar built a library of 24,000 books including rare and precious manuscripts that he had either inherited, won in battle or commissioned. He also established a Bureau of Translations where books in various languages were translated into Persian, including major Hindu books such as the Ramayana, the Mahabharata and the Harivamsa (Krishna's life).

There were many scholars at Akbar's court who were proficient in more than one language, such as Badauni, who did a lot of translation work. Birbal, too, spoke fluent Persian as well as Hindi and Sanskrit. He is credited with translating the Bhagavad Gita.

Akbar's other interests included pigeon-flying and *chaughan*, a form of polo. Birbal, too, enjoyed playing polo.

Siva Alone is Real

The Chola King Vikrama was a fanatical Saivite. He was angry that some Vaishnavaites of Ramanuja's cult were asserting that Vishnu was superior to Siva. To put down this heresy, he had the formula 'Siva is Supreme. He is the one and only Eternal verity. Nothing is superior to him', written in a register. He compelled every worshipper of Vishnu to subscribe to it on pain of blinding or death. A great Vaishnava sage went to the court in answer to the king's summons. When required to subscribe to the formula, he asked, 'Sire, will this register containing this formula last unto eternity?' 'Certainly not,' said the king, 'it will not last more than two or three hundred years at the most.' 'Your Majesty, is it fitting to proclaim Siva's eternity and supremacy in anything not eternal?' asked the sage. The king allowed the validity of the objection and discontinued his persecution of those who would not subscribe to the formula.

Mother Tongue

At Akbar's court, there were many scholars learned in more than one language. Some knew Arabic, the language of the holy Koran. Others spoke Turki, the language of Akbar's ancestors. There were men who understood Sanskrit, in which the Hindu holy books are written. Of course, everyone spoke Persian, the official language of the court.

One day, a traveller arrived at Akbar's palace. He spoke Arabic, Persian, Turki, Sanskrit and even Chinese and Latin. The king's scholars were astonished by his linguistic abilities. He could hold a fluent conversation with them in any of the languages in which they specialised. No one could detect any mistakes or even the trace of an accent in his speech.

Akbar was impressed by this talented stranger and wanted to know more about him. 'Which country are you from originally? What is your mother tongue?'

But the mysterious stranger would not tell. 'That is for me to know, and you to find out!'

Akbar turned to Birbal. 'Birbal, surely you have guessed by now where this man is from?'

Birbal had been observing and listening to the newcomer closely since he had arrived, but he said, 'I need a little more time, Your Majesty. You will know by tomorrow.'

That night, Birbal, accompanied by one of his servants, went to the stranger's room secretly. He hid himself near the bedroom window, while his servant went in and sprinkled some cold water on the sleeping man. Startled, the man awoke and exclaimed in an angry voice. When he went back to sleep, Birbal and his servant returned quietly to their home.

The next morning, Birbal announced to the emperor:

'Your Majesty; our mysterious friend is from Gujarat.'

The stranger was speechless in amazement. 'But...but how did you know?'

Birbal smiled. 'Forgive me, stranger, but I startled you in your sleep last night. Unwittingly, you yelled out some Gujarati words. No matter how many languages they may speak, when surprised or in pain, men usually use their mother tongue.'

Akbar and the other courtiers broke into applause as the stranger bowed to Birbal in admiration.

Precept Broken

Dadaji Kondadev, the Brahmin tutor of Sivaji, was a great exponent of bourgeois honesty. He planted a mango garden for his master Shahji, Sivaji's father, and said that he would cut off the arm of anybody who removed a mango from there. When the trees bore fruit, the fruits were so tempting that forgetting his own previous saying, he plucked a fruit which had ripened on the tree. Just as he did so, he remembered his previous saying and wanted to cut off his own arm. Sivaji and Jiji Bai begged him not to do so, and added, 'We order you not to do so.' Dadaji finally obeyed, but kept an iron collar round his neck to show that he was a thief.

But all his efforts to make his pupil Sivaji conform to the same Spartan code of bourgeois honesty failed. Sivaji plundered Bijapur villages, plundered Surat, plundered Khandesh and other Mughal territories and never felt so happy as when he was taking away those plundered properties. One day, a friend deferentially asked Sivaji what he thought of Dadaji's ideal. 'Very good in a servant content with his lot; but not so good in a ruler anxious to regain his people's liberty.' said Sivaji. 'Had I followed his advice I would have obeyed Bijapur, and obeyed the Mughals, and never freed the Hindus or Maharashtra. Dear Dadaji's precepts have been broken, but Hinduism has been saved thereby. Even merchants, like the East India Co. aspiring to be masters, have shaken off this bourgeois honesty. That is why they offered to buy the six thousand rupees worth of clothes looted from Surat provided they were not overrated but cheap and good. In other words, honesty was the best policy, but was to be abandoned when dishonesty paid better. With poor Dadaji, honesty was not a policy but a principle, and he would never have bought those clothes at any price. So, the East India company is sure to build a great empire one day, whereas Dadaji spent all his days in subjection.'

A Song Story

Akbar loved to listen to stories. He hired readers whose only work was to read books aloud to the king. He especially loved exciting tales full of danger and action. If he had had a hard day hunting or riding, he would sometimes fall asleep and start snoring before the story was over. Then the reader would quietly snuff out the lamp and leave the royal bedchamber. But if the king had spent the day doing tedious and boring things, then he would be wide awake and alert at bedtime, waiting to be entertained.

On one particular night, it was Birbal's turn to tell Akbar a story. The king was in the mood for a really long story while Birbal was tired and sleepy. But, naturally, Birbal could not back out of his duties to his royal master. He stifled his yawn and began to spin a yarn.

'I've already heard this one, Birbal. Tell me a new one.'

Birbal racked his brains to think of a tale he had not already told Akbar. His tired mind could not come up with anything. He decided to make up a story on the spot and also cure Akbar of this tedious habit.

'Once upon a time,' Birbal began, 'a farmer had a granary made where he could store the grain harvested from his field. It was important that the shed be absolutely airtight without any opening, so that the grain would remain fresh. But after the granary had been built and the wheat had been stored, one small problem remained.'

Akbar sat up in bed. 'What was that?' he asked eagerly. Perhaps the story would turn out to be an exciting one.

'Well, the builders didn't do a really good job,' Birbal continued. 'A tiny hole remained at the top of the shed. It was large enough to allow a sparrow to enter. The bird carried off a grain of wheat. It told the other sparrows about it. Next, one more sparrow came and took a grain in its beak.'

'Then what happened?' asked the emperor.

'Another sparrow came and carried off a grain of wheat.'

'And then?'

'One more sparrow flew off with a grain of wheat from the granary.'

'But what happened next?'

Birbal described how each bird carried away a grain of wheat. By the time he had repeated the same sentence fifty times, Akbar had become really impatient. 'But I want to know what happened next in the story! I've heard enough about the sparrows.'

'But, Your Majesty, thousands and thousands of birds came to that granary and carried off a grain of wheat in their beaks. I have only told you about a few. The story cannot move on until every single grain of wheat has been removed. It may take several months or years to complete this story.'

'Enough, enough!' grumbled the disgruntled king. 'I don't want to hear any more of this boring tale. Leave me alone. I want to sleep.'

Happy to be relieved of his duty, Birbal snuffed out the lamp and tiptoed out of the emperor's bedroom.

Come an Hour Earlier

Sivaji swooped on Surat in 1664 with four thousand men. Two rajas, eager for a share in the plunder, joined him with six thousand men. The governor of Surat and the three richest merchants, Haji Said Beg, Baharji Borah and Haji Qasim, refused to meet Sivaji for a parley as requested by him. He had wanted them to meet him in order to settle the terms on which he would spare Surat from fire and sword. As no parley was held and no terms settled, Sivaji's men plundered and burnt as they pleased. The governor and the big men left the town undefended and retired to the castle against which Sivaji organised a mock attack by musketeers to keep the inmates in a state of fright.

For three days the Mahrattas sacked, burnt, plundered and destroyed two-thirds of the town, turning the days into nights by the columns of smoke, and the nights into days by the blazing fires. Baharji Borah's shop was looted and burnt. Haji Said Beg's residence and warehouse were also looted in part. Then some quicksilver cask was broken open and the quicksilver spilt on the floor. Some of the Mahrattas set fire to an adjoining house which was in close proximity to the English factory. The English were afraid that the conflagration would spread to their factory and so made a sortie against the twenty-five horsemen in the street doing the mischief. One of the Mahrattas was wounded by a bullet, and two Englishmen with arrows and sword. The English put a guard the next day over Haji Said Beg's house and prevented further looting. Sivaji was angry and sent the English a message on Friday afternoon asking them to pay him three hundred thousand rupees or to leave Haji Said Beg's house so that he might loot it in full. He added that if they did neither, he would lead his troops in person against their factory and kill every soul therein and raze the factory to the ground.

President Oxenden and his council took time till Saturday morning to consider the demands, and then sent the following reply. 'Come an hour earlier than you intended. You shall find us ready to meet you. We shall not run away.' The challenging reply had its intended effect. Sivaji fretted and fumed. When his captains suggested an immediate attack on the insolent foreigners, he replied 'No. We are no longer hungry cobras ready for a fray, but over-fed pythons surfeited with loot. We have enormous booty to carry home and cannot waste out time over these desperate men with their scanty belongings which they will bravely defend with their last drop of blood.'

The Five Greatest Fools in Agra

Akbar was tired of the endless debates in his court. He was sick of listening to wise men and scholars. They were so serious and boring. He wanted to have some fun for a change. He decided he wanted to listen to some fools instead.

Akbar summoned Birbal. 'Tomorrow morning, I want you to go into Agra and find me the five biggest fools in the city. Bring them to my palace by the end of the day.'

Birbal was neither surprised nor taken aback by this strange request. He knew the king was in a strange mood. He knew better than to argue with him. He bowed low, and touched his head with his right palm, as was the customary greeting for servants to the king. 'But of course, Your Majesty. Your wish is my command. By the end of the day tomorrow, you will have your five fools.'

Next morning, at sunrise, Birbal set off for the city. He didn't have any idea how to find fools. He decided to walk around in the more crowded part of the town. The more people there were to look at, the better were his chances of finding a fool. He sat down in a corner of the bazaar and waited.

Before long, he saw a curious sight. Along came a woodcutter, seated on a donkey, carrying a bundle of wood on his head. He could have strapped it behind him on the donkey.

Birbal hastened to the woodcutter's side. 'Excuse my curiosity, sir, but could you tell me why you carry your burden on your head, when you have such a fine donkey to carry it for you?'

The woodcutter was delighted to have such a refined gentleman address him, a mere woodcutter, as 'sir'.

'This good donkey has worked for me all his life. Now he is old and feeble. I do not wish to give him too heavy a load to bear. So, although I sit on his back, I carry the wood I have chopped on my own heads.'

Birbal stifled a smile. Here was his first fool. He said to the man, 'How wonderful to meet a man as kind as you in these otherwise cruel times. Although he is a beast of burden, you share your donkey's load. How lucky he is to have a master like you. Come with me, kind sir, and I will make sure that neither you nor your donkey carries a heavy load ever again.'

The woodcutter, pleased to be getting so much attention from the polite gentleman, readily agreed to follow him around town. So, Birbal, the woodcutter and his donkey wandered about looking for more fools.

Suddenly Birbal stopped short. There in the middle of the path in front of them lay a man, flat on his back. He was cycling his legs in the air and he held both his arms straight up and stiffly apart.

Birbal went up to the man. 'What are you doing lying on the ground like that? Our donkey almost stepped upon you. Why don't you stand up?'

'Help me stand up,' the man gasped. 'I slipped and fell and now I cannot rise without using my hands.'

'Then why don't you use your hands to help yourself? Why do you hold them up in the air like that?'

'Questions, questions,' grumbled the man. 'Are you going to help me up or not?'

'Very well,' said Birbal, and pulled the man to his feet. He continued to hold his arms straight out in front of him.

'You must tell me why you hold your arms in that position,' Birbal insisted, his curiosity thoroughly aroused.

'Well, sire, this morning my wife sent me to the bazaar to buy a measure of cloth. This is how much cloth she wants me to buy,' the man said, emphasizing the distance between his hands. 'If I put my arms down, how will I remember how much cloth she wanted? You don't know my wife, sire. She would not be pleased if I did not buy the right amount of fabric.'

'Aha!' Birbal exclaimed, highly entertained by the story and happy to have found another fool. 'So that is the reason for your strange posture. How fortunate your wife is to have a husband that obeys her so well. Come with me today, and your wife will have as much fabric as her heart desires for the rest of her life.'

And the dutiful husband happily joined Birbal and the woodcutter as they walked through the city looking for more fools. But fools weren't that easy to come by. Most people in Agra were quite clever. The day passed, it started getting dark, and Birbal still hadn't found another fool.

Suddenly, he saw a strange sight. By the flaming torch which served as street lighting was a full grown man, crawling about on his hands and knees like a baby. This looked very promising!

Birbal ran up to the man. 'What are you doing crawling around in the dust like that, good sir? Your fine white silken clothes will get all messed up!'

The man, who looked as though he were a prosperous merchant, looked up. 'I lost my diamond ring when I was chatting with some friends this afternoon. I have a habit of twisting it about on my finger, and it must have fallen off. I only just discovered my loss and came back to look for it.'

'A diamond ring!' exclaimed Birbal. 'It must have been

quite expensive. Perhaps we can all help you look for it. Do you remember exactly where you were standing when you were chatting with your friends?'

Pleased with the attention of the sympathetic stranger, the merchant pointed to a clump of trees a short distance away. 'We were standing under the shade of the trees in the hot afternoon.'

Birbal was astonished. 'If you lost your ring there under the trees, then why are you looking for it here, so far away?'

The merchant was quite irritated by Birbal's failure to understand the obvious.'It is completely dark under the trees. How do you expect me to find a small ring in the dark?! I am looking for it under the streetlight because I can see clearly here.'

Birbal struck his forehead with his palm. 'But of course! How foolish of me to ask such a silly question! But, noble sir, you seem tired and dusty. Accompany me and I shall obtain for you not one diamond ring, but two.'

The merchant agreed to go with Birbal. He had looked long enough for his ring, and now he might get two for free. He had nothing to lose.

Birbal was exhausted by now with his day-long excursion in the city He turned towards the palace with his three fools.

One by one, he presented the fools to the emperor. Akbar light-heartedly heard each one's story. He gave each man two handfuls of gold coins, more than enough to buy what Birbal had promised them. He was about to reward Birbal when he stopped short.

'Birbal, I asked you for five fools. But you have only brought me three. Where are the other two fools?'

Birbal bowed his head and humbly touched it with his right palm. 'Your Majesty, the fourth fool is I, for having gone on such a foolish mission.'

Akbar stifled a smile. He could see what Birbal was getting at. 'And the fifth fool, Birbal. Dare I ask who the fifth fool is?'

At this Birbal prostrated himself flat on the floor, and placed the emperor's feet upon his head. Then he kissed the royal feet and stood up.

'May the sun and the moon revolve around you! May you live for a thousand years! May the world sing your praises for another ten thousand years! But if Your Majesty will forgive this worthless servant's impertinence—may I dare to humbly suggest, that the fifth fool is you for having sent me on such a foolish mission.'

Akbar laughed until the tears ran down his cheeks. Then he clasped Birbal to him in a big embrace. 'This is why I love you, Birbal. You can make me laugh and forget for a moment how important I am!'

The Flag of God

Sivaji made Ramdas his guru and installed him in Sajjangarh and gave him money and jewels in order to save him from begging from the faithful every day. But, to his surprise, he found the guru still going on his daily rounds. So, thinking that he had not given enough, he, in a mood of religious ecstasy, placed at his feet a deed gifting his whole kingdom and all its treasury and future income. Ramdas accepted the gift and made Sivaji his agent, saying, 'Child, hereafter nothing belongs to you. It is all God's property. So, manage everything as a trustee on my behalf.' 'With pleasure,' said Sivaji. 'I hope your holiness will not hereafter go on your begging rounds.' 'Oh, I can't desist from that,' said Ramdas. 'Why?' asked Sivaji. 'Because I must see if the people think that I deserve my meal every day or not. They give me food because they think that I have enough fire in my belly to burn all their sins up. When I cease to fulfil their expectations, I must be prepared to starve as my mission would have been over. The moment they cease to give me enough to keep me alive, I shall know that my days of usefulness are over. All public men and public institutions should always be subjected to such an acid test every day to prevent inward rottenness.'

Sivaji was impressed. Next day, he adopted the ochre flag called '*Bhagwan Jhanda*' or 'God's Flag'. His ministers asked him, 'Why this colour?' He replied, 'That is my master's flag and will make me aware that I am ever in the eyes of God. My

people shall know thereby that, at the call of duty, I am prepared
to renounce everything for them.'

Years passed. Sivaji had a premonition of his approaching
death. He called his queens, his sons Shambhaji and Rajaram,
his premier Trimbak, and his viceroy Annajai Datto. He showed
Shambhaji his treasury, revenue returns and lists of forts and
troops and urged him to be worthy of such a rich heritage and of
the flag of God and to be true to all the high hopes entertained
by the Hindus. 'Don't quarrel with your brother or stepmother,'
said he. 'Be impartial between Brahmins and Kayasths. Avoid
magicians and quack physicians. I shall die soon, and you will
be all alone to protect the flag.' 'There is little to fear,' said
Trimbak. 'Your Majesty has made the Mughals tremble. There
is no danger of their conquering us anymore.'

'No, not much to fear from them,' said Sivaji. 'The flame
lighted by me will prove too much for them to extinguish.
Indeed, they will present no problem a century hence. You have
little to fear from them.' 'Then, from whom? From the decadent
Bijapuris?' asked Shambhaji. 'No' said Sivaji. 'My fears are not
of them'. 'Then whom do you fear, father?' asked Shambhaji.

'My fears are only about ourselves. I fear quarrels between
you Shambhu and Rajaram. I fear feuds between you Shambhu
and Rajaram. I fear feuds between the queens. I fear our own
people, caste-proud Brahmins and caste-conscious Kayasths
and Mahrattas. I fear feuds between Trimbak and Annaji. Our
greatest fears are about ourselves,' said Sivaji.

'We shall see that these feuds are brought under control,'
said Trimbak. 'So Your Majesty may die in peace'.

'I fear not for myself', said Sivaji. 'The body is burnt, the
soul is immortal. I fear for you and the Hindu race and our flag.
The work is far greater than I thought. Defeating non-Hindu foes

is not so difficult. Defeating our own foes from inside is a far greater problem. One Sivaji cannot save the Hindu race. Nor is one generation enough. Many men and many generations are required to save this race.' 'The Hindu race will surely be saved some day and Your Majesty's work completed', said Trimbak. 'It is a pity Your Majesty will not live long enough to see it.' 'Perhaps it is for the best,' said Sivaji. 'The Hindu race can only be saved by sacrificing many essentially Hindu things which I love and pride in. Caste, for instance, may have to be sacrificed at the altar of the Mother, and I may not like it. I must leave the problem of saving the Hindus to others and concentrate now on saving myself. Bring the flag of God and place it before my eyes. Let the Brahmins recite the Vedas and the Gita, and let the last rites be carried out.' That was done, and Sivaji exclaimed in a low voice, 'The flag of God is waving gaily. I shall follow it.' Then he sank into unconsciousness and passed away to the great land of peace.

It's All for the Best

A king heard of a famous Brahmin astrologer. He wanted to
test him. He sent for him one evening. Holding in his closed
fist three cat's eye stones, he asked the astrologer, 'What have
I in my hand?' The latter did not know what to say. If he said
anything wrong, not only would his chance of getting service
under such a generous king disappear, but his reputation itself
would be gone. In his confusion he simply looked at the hall
vacantly and saw a cat's eye gleaming at him from the darkness.
'Cat's eye,' he murmured mechanically. 'That is right.' said the
king astonished. 'How many?' Encouraged by his previous luck,
the astrologer watched for signs. A conch was sounded thrice
in a temple close by. The astrologer said 'Three.' 'Quite right,'
said the king, and made him court astrologer and inseparable
companion.

   The astrologer, because of his great luck in the original test,
took as his stock phrase, 'It is for the best.' A year after he had
taken service, the king was cleaning his swords preliminary to
go out for a hunt in the hills. Accidentally he cut off the tip of
his left index finger which bled freely. He yelled with pain and
showed it to the astrologer who remarked, 'It is for the best.'
'Put out at this callous repetition of the stock phrase,' the king
told him. 'Get out of here, and don't let me see your face again.'
The astrologer went away remarking, 'It is for the best.' The
king bit his lips and wondered at the man's coolness.

Later in the day, the king went out to hunt. In his ardour, he went far ahead of his men and was soon alone in a dark forest. He was weary and thristy. There lived in that forest a gang of terrible devotees of Kali who wanted to offer a human sacrifice to that dread deity to gain their ends. They were in search of a suitable man, preferably a king or a Brahmin. They were overjoyed at seeing the king alone, weary and helpless and caught him. 'It is the goddess's gift,' said the head of these fanatics. 'He seems to be perfect. Examine him carefully though, for nobody with the least defect in limb can be offered to great Kali.' His followers examined the king and saw the defective finger. 'Leave the man. He won't do for the goddess,' said the head. So the gang released the king and went away.

The king was overjoyed at his providential escape. Some hours later, his men came and joined him. When he returned to the palace, he sent for the astrologer and said, 'I apologize for my ungrateful conduct. It was indeed for the best that I cut my finger. Else, I would have been offered up in sacrifice by the demon. But, tell me why you said when you were sent away in disgrace that that was also for the best.'

'Can't you see?' asked the astrologer, 'you always take me with you wherever you go. Had you not sent me away that day, I would have accompanied you for the hunt and those devotees of Kali would have offered me in sacrifice, as I am a Brahmin and with no defective limbs. Truly, it was the best thing that could have happened to me.'

The king laughed, gave the astrologer a purse of gold, and restored him to rank and favour.

The Perfect Portrait

Many of Akbar's nobles were inspired by the emperor's interest in painting. They also employed artists to paint pictures and portraits for them. Many gifted and talented painters worked in Akbar's capital.

One day, a noble asked a young painter in court to paint an exact likeness of him. The painter was not that well-known as yet and wanted an opportunity to impress important people at court with his work. He hoped that the emperor would then give him a chance to work on a more important project. He was delighted to have been approached, and quickly painted a portrait of the noble and brought it back to him.

He found that the noble had just shaved off his beard. 'What sort of a portrait is this? I asked for an exact likeness! Look at me—do I have a beard?'

'But you did when you sat for the portrait, sire,' the artist countered.

The noble would not be appeased. Afraid that he would be considered incompetent, the painter immediately agreed to re-do the picture. This time, when he presented the completed portrait, the noble had just shaved off his moustache.

'Is this what you call an exact likeness?! Do I have a moustache?'

It was pointless to argue that he had had a moustache when he sat for the portrait. The poor painter re-did the picture. Five times, he painted the noble's portrait. Five times the noble changed his appearance in some way so that the painting would not be an exact likeness of him. The struggling young artist became sad and frustrated. It appeared his career at court would be ruined by this capricious noble. He went to Birbal and asked for his help.

Birbal listened to the whole story. He suggested that the painter ask for one last chance. He then told him how to teach the man a lesson. This time, when he went to present the completed portrait to the noble, Birbal accompanied him. As the noble waited smugly, ready to pounce on some inaccuracy, the artist handed him a mirror.

'What is this? This is not a painting! It is just a mirror.'

'Precisely, sire. The only way you can obtain an exact likeness of yourself is if you look at yourself in the mirror. You do not need an artist. There is no art involved.'

Shamefaced, the noble had to concede that the young man was indeed a talented artist and had to pay him for all the portraits he had painted of him. Thanks to Birbal, the painter's reputation was saved. He even went on to become quite well known as a portrait painter.

The King and His Critic

Long long ago, there was a king who was reputed to be one of the best kings that any country ever had. There lived in his dominion a critic who was criticising the king's actions and even intentions fearlessly. The king did not like the critic at all and secretly resolved to wreak his vengenance on him one day. After twenty-five years of beneficent rule, the king felt himself powerful enough to punish the critic. He ordered that poor man to be hanged for a highly critical article on his reign published on the silver jubilee day when the subjects were wild with enthusiasm for the king. The man sought and obtained a last minute interview with the king. The latter went near the condemned man and asked him what he had done to merit death. 'What good did you ever do to your king or country?' asked the king, 'and what good will it do to either of them if you were saved from the gallows?' 'Sire,' replied the critic, 'my constant criticism made you ever watchful, and saved the country from all possible injustice. It has made you one of the best kings who have ruled this land. This much I did for my king and country. If I were saved from the gallows, my king will retain his name unsullied, and my country will not lose the faculty of fearless criticism. If you can lay your hands on your breast and declare that what I say just now is false, you are welcome to hang me. Otherwise, your majesty will be pleased to release me.' 'Release him,' said the king, turning away from the critic and shedding a tear of repentance, 'release him, for he is speaking the truth.'

The Flatterer

One day, a poet from a distant place arrived at Akbar's court. The king was interested in traveller's tales and also enjoyed fine poetry. He was so pleased with the visitor's songs and poems that he gave him a rich reward—a huge bag of gold. The poet was so overwhelmed by the king's generosity that he begged permission to compose a poem in his praise.

'You are the greatest king in Hindustan, Your Majesty. No other king in this land has a kingdom as big as yours, a heart as generous!'

Akbar smiled, quite pleased. He knew this was true. He was definitely the most important king in India in those days.

The flatterer continued, bowing low as he spoke. 'In fact, you are the greatest king in this world, Your Majesty. No other king in the world has a kingdom as powerful as yours. No other emperor has as many palaces or as magnificent a court as yours!'

Akbar nodded and smiled. Although he had not seen the world, he had visitors from other lands attend his court and he knew that his fame had spread far and wide. He was pleased at the flatterer's words. Everyone in the court was listening, including some foreign visitors. He decided to bestow an even greater reward on his eloquent admirer.

Pleased at the effect he was having on the emperor, the poet continued, 'In fact, Your Majesty, the sun and the moon and the stars revolve around you…because you are the greatest king in the universe—greater even than Lord Indra!'

He had gone too far. There was a stunned silence in the court. Lord Indra was the King of all gods, the highest god for Hindus. All the nobles—Hindus and Muslims, as well as the foreign visitors who were Christians—believed that no man could rival the greatness of God. Akbar, too, was taken aback by the man's words. But he was amused by the shocked looks on all the faces around him.

He looked around the hall. 'Well, what do you all think? Am I greater than God? No one is contradicting the man. Does that mean you agree with him?'

The nobles began to shift and shuffle uncomfortably. They did not wish to be blasphemous. Yet, how could they tell the emperor without offending him that neither he nor any man was greater than God?

'If you agree that I am greater than God, then give me one reason why you think so.'

Akbar looked at his courtiers turn by turn. The men either lowered their eyes or coughed to hide their embarrassment. No one had the courage to answer his question truthfully and risk his displeasure.

Akbar turned to Birbal. 'Well, Birbal, do you think I am greater than God?'

Unhesitatingly, Birbal replied, 'Undoubtedly, Your Majesty! Of course you are greater than God!'

'And why is that, Birbal?'

'Your Majesty there is certainly one thing that you can do that God cannot.'

'And what is that, Birbal?' Akbar waited eagerly to see what Birbal would say. The other nobles watched to see how Birbal would get himself out of this embarrassing situation without offending the emperor.

'Majesty, it you wish to banish a man, all you have to do is send him out of your kingdom. But if God, whose kingdom is the universe, wishes to banish a man... He has nowhere to send him! Therefore, I repeat, Your Majesty, you are greater than God, because you can do one thing that He cannot do.'

Akbar was pleased at the tactful way Birbal had put him in his place. By reminding him that his kingdom had limits, while God's kingdom had none, Birbal had pointed out the infinite superiority of the Creator, but without insulting his emperor.

Akbar laughed delightedly. The nobles smiled and nervously wiped the sweat off their faces. Birbal had saved them all from a very tricky situation.

Akbar's World

The kings who ruled Delhi before the Mughals had large numbers of wives living in strict seclusion in special parts of the palace called the harem. They had to veil themselves in front of males other than their husbands and close relatives. This practice of veiling was known as *parda*.

Akbar also had an enormous harem. It is said that he had more than 300 wives, though less than a dozen are mentioned by name in history books. Many of the marriages were political alliances with other royal families to ensure peace and harmony among the rulers. Akbar married at least six Hindu princesses for this reason.

Akbar's harem contained more than 5,000 women. But not all of these were the king's wives or concubines. Other women related to the royal family—widowed aunts, unmarried sisters and cousins—also lived there along with their many maids. Each wife had a separate apartment and received a salary for her expenditure. Female superintendents supervised the different sections of the harem. It was zealously guarded. When other women, relatives or wives of nobles, wished to visit their friends inside the royal harem, they had to apply for permission.

Women had opportunities to learn languages such as Persian and Sanskrit, as well as fine art and literature. Parties of royal women went on pilgrimages every month. They also frequently accompanied the king on his travels to distant lands.

Royal women lived in a world of their own. Although they could not be seen by other men, they could observe a great deal from behind screened walls. They also had direct access to the king, who spent at least a few hours every day in the harem, and could influence his decisions. The king's mother was exceptionally important and had a higher position than his chief wife.

Royal children were especially pampered and coddled by the many loving females around them, not just their own mothers. Queens had many helpers and did not physically have to take care of their babies. Akbar had many wet nurses, or ayahs, when he was born. When he was separated from his parents for two years as a toddler, it was his nurses who looked after him.

When Akbar was four years, four months and four days old, he was scheduled to start his schooling at an auspicious hour chosen by astrologers, but he was nowhere to be found; he had run off to play! Akbar's father Humayun appointed teacher after teacher as he grew older, but the young prince was just not interested in studying. He preferred to spend his time flying pigeons, observing animals and hunting.

Yet, Akbar showed the signs of being an imperious ruler even as a child. His admirers claimed that by remaining unschooled, Akbar had been able to nurture the greatness within him. He did learn to read eventually but never liked to write. Despite his initial resistance to education, he later developed a tremendous respect for knowledge and gathered many learned scholars about him.

The King's Review

It was a custom in an ancient Hindu kingdom that a king should, on his coronation day, review the army in order to find out whether it was keeping up its courage and efficiency.

Kirtivarman held the usual coronation day review in the way laid down by custom and precedent. He picked out a soldier at random and asked him to climb up a tree forty feet high and jump down. Without the slightest hesitation, the soldier did as he was ordered, and so met with instant death. The king gave a handsome pension to the deceased man's wife and relations for life, ordered for the dead soldier a cremation with full military honours, announced that the soldiers retained all their ancient courage and efficiency, and declared the review over.

A foreign visitor was shocked at the seemingly cruel order of the king and told him that the whole thing was barbarous in the extreme. 'No,' replied Kirtivarman, 'this is not more barbarous than war in general. War implies implicit obedience to command, undaunted bravery, and readiness to die at a moment's notice. All these were tested now by selecting one man at random, and his relations are rewarded. Some kings indulge in bloody wars involving the loss of countless lives in order to keep their soldiers fit. I keep my soldiers fit by an occasional sacrifice of one life. So long as the demon of war remains, this is inevitable.'

Appeasing the Begum

One of Akbar's wives had a brother that she doted on. She felt that he was one of the most capable men at court. And yet, her husband, the emperor, did not give him a position worthy of his qualities. Instead Birbal seemed to get undue favours and importance. She decided to take the matter up with her husband one more time.

'But, Begum,' the king pleaded, 'I need intelligent men running the affairs of the country. Your brother is a good man, but he just doesn't have what it takes to hold a really important position.'

'How about Birbal?' she countered. 'You just like him because he is funny. How can you justify entrusting a mere jester with such important responsibilities?'

'Birbal is not a mere jester, as you put it, Begum,' the king explained patiently. 'He is a very wise and intelligent man. He is so clever that I truly doubt there is anything he cannot do.'

The begum saw her chance. 'Very well, let us set Birbal an impossible task. If he is unable to perform it, then you give his position at court to my brother.'

Akbar did not wish to displease his pretty wife. She was his current favourite and he did not want her to sulk. Besides, he was completely confident that Birbal could do anything. 'Anything to please you, my pretty one. You suggest the task Birbal should perform.'

'Tomorrow when you are strolling in the garden, ask Birbal to fetch me. I will refuse to come. He will fail for sure.' She smiled triumphantly. Already she could imagine her brother being appointed as an important man at court.

The next day, the emperor was taking his evening stroll in the garden. He turned to Birhal and said, 'My begum is angry with me and refuses to see me. Please go and persuade her to join me. Only you can put her in a better mood.'

As Birbal turned to leave and do his king's bidding, the emperor added: 'Oh, and, Birbal, I should tell you that if you do not succeed in bringing her to me, I will have to give your post to the begum's brother. That would please her immensely.'

Birbal immediately understood what had happened. He never underestimated the power of the women in the harem. Thank goodness the emperor had warned him. Birbal knew that Akbar could not stand the begum's brother, and would never want him in his circle of trusted advisors, but he must have been forced by his wife into making a promise. Birbal realised he had to make sure the begum went to see the emperor. His job depended on it.

He arrived in the harem and asked to be presented to the begum. The begum, of course, was waiting for him. She was eager to see him fail.

Birbal bowed low. 'Your Highness, I have an important message for you from the emperor. He is in the palace garden and wants you to...'

Just then, a servant entered and went up to Birbal. He whispered something in his ear. The begum could not hear what he said, but three words caught her attention: 'She is beautiful'.

Birbal's expression changed to one of embarrassment. He sent the servant away and turned to the begum. 'Things have changed, Your Highness. Please do not bother to come to the garden. His Majesty has other things to attend to.' He bowed and quickly left the room.

When he had gone, the begum began to worry. Why had Akbar changed his mind about inviting her to the garden? Those three words she had overheard— 'she is beautiful'—troubled her greatly. Could it be that the king was meeting another beautiful woman in the garden? She was his favourite at the moment, but the begum knew how easily the emperor could shift his attention to another woman. The harem was full of women who no longer interested the king. The begum did not want to become one of them. She decided that she would not allow another woman to take away her place beside the emperor.

Hurriedly, the begum made her way to the garden, where Akbar waited alone. He raised his eyebrows in surprise. 'But, Begum, you swore that you would not come when I called you. What made you change your mind?'

The begum looked around the garden. Besides the king's attendants, there was no one else present. No beautiful woman. She realised that Birbal had fooled her by making her jealous.

'Your Birbal tricked me into coming here,' she said furiously.

'Did he tell you a lie? If he did, I will punish him.'

But Birbal had managed to manipulate her without actually telling a lie. Just through the power of suggestion he had shrewdly used her innermost fears to make her jealous and arouse her curiosity. But the begum could not admit to the emperor that she had been tricked into coming because she thought he was meeting another woman.

Birbal appeared a few minutes later and saluted the king and queen. Akbar smiled happily, relieved that he would not have to put up with the begum's insufferably pompous brother after all. 'Bravo, Birbal. I always said you could accomplish the impossible!'

The queen looked at the ground and said nothing. Reluctantly, she had to admit that Birbal was intelligent, with a deep understanding of human nature.

The Powers of Children

One morning, Birbal arrived late in court. The emperor had been waiting impatiently for him. 'Why are you late, Birbal? You know I do not like to be kept waiting.'

'A million apologies, Your Majesty! Normally I never allow anything to keep me from my duties. But today…well, it was just unavoidable.'

Akbar wouldn't let it go at that. His curiosity was aroused. 'But what happened, Birbal? What was important enough to keep you from your king?'

Surprisingly, Birbal, who always had a smooth and prompt answer for everything, seemed embarrassed. He didn't want to discuss the matter in front of the other nobles. But when Akbar persisted in probing, he finally admitted: 'Well, Majesty, it was my little grandson. His toy was broken and he wouldn't let me leave the house until I had fixed it for him.'

Akbar was flabbergasted. 'You allowed a mere child to get the better of you! Why, you are an adult! Surely you could have reasoned with him and explained that you would fix it later.'

'But, Majesty, one can't reason with a little child who is throwing a tantrum. Children are powerful creatures. They can humble the greatest adults if they wish.'

Akbar was not convinced. 'Bring your grandchild to court this minute. I will show you how to handle him.'

Birbal obediently fetched his two-year-old grandson into the emperor's presence. The toddler smiled sweetly at the king, and even agreed to come and sit in his lap.

Akbar looked triumphantly at Birbal. 'See how well I handle him. I have many grandchildren of my own.'

Then the boy began to fidget and shift, 'I'm hungry now,' he said, looking up at the king.

'What would you like to eat?' the emperor asked kindly.

The child thought for a moment. 'Sugar cane,' he said.

Attendants immediately brought in sugar cane that had been cut into tiny child-sized pieces.

The toddler refused to eat any of it. 'No-no, not like that, I want the big sugar cane.'

Akbar snapped his fingers and his servants brought in a large stick of sugar cane that had not been cut up. But even this did not please the child.

He began to sniffle. 'I want all the little pieces to be put back together to make a big one, like it used to be.'

'But that is impossible, child!' The emperor was beginning to get impatient. 'No one can join together a sugar cane that has been chopped up.'

'That's what I want. I will eat only that. Put it back together again this instant.' The boy stamped his foot and began to cry.

Desperately, the emperor tried to comfort him and distract him with other foods. Plates and plates of colourful and delicious sweets were brought in for the child. Then all kinds of fruits. But the child wouldn't have any of it. His wails grew louder and louder.

Akbar threw up his hands in defeat and handed the crying child back to his grandfather. 'I suppose you were right Birbal. You cannot reason with small children, and therein lies their power. They can humble even the greatest adults.'

A Princess's Choice

Kumaradevi, the beautiful daughter of the Lichchhavis, announced her intention to select a husband for herself. All the princes, nobles and rich men of India flocked to Vaisali in order not to miss a chance of winning the handsomest and most accomplished princess of the age. All the suitors were led to the grand dining hall to partake of a sumptuous feast. Kumaradevi came there with the marriage garland. She asked the guests one by one what their qualifications to sit at the feast were. Some said that they were kings, others that they were princes, others that they were big merchants, others that they were mighty generals, others that they were statesmen, and others that they were famous scholars. When she put the question to the young prince Chandragupta, he replied, 'I am hungry, and that is my best qualification for sitting at this feast.' Kumaradevi was highly pleased with the reply, but wanted to ask two questions more. She asked all the suitors how they would treat her if she married them. One said, 'As my goddess'; another said 'As my monitor in everything'; another said 'As my greatest treasure'; another said 'I shall be your slave'; she asked Chandragupta, and he said, 'I shall treat you as my wedded wife and helpmate in all my duties. I shall not be your slave or expect you to be mine. We shall both retain our free minds uncurbed, and shall, by frank discussion and mutual consultation, advance our welfare and that of our progeny and subjects.' The princess beamed with pleasure. Then she asked the third question to all the suitors. 'What will you give me if I marry you?' 'All my kingdom,' said one. 'The most wonderful string of pearls in the world,' said another. 'New delicacies every day,' said a third. 'The finest dresses,' said a fourth. 'Thousands of maid-servants to wait on you,' said a fifth. 'Chariots with horses, fleet as the sun,' said a sixth. She asked Chandragupta, and he replied, 'My heart's love and a son worthy of you.' Blushing she put the marriage garland round his neck saying, 'You are indeed the husband meant for me; what does a woman prize higher than a loving husband and a glorious son?'

Lilavathi's Corroboration

Lilavathi, the celebrated lady mathematician of ancient India, with her father, the even more famous mathematician Bhaskaracharya, was one day attending the court of a local king. She was then only a girl of ten, but so great was her reputation for common sense and learning that the king and his ministers used to listen to her words with as much respect as to those of learned pundits. One day, a great noble told the king and the courtiers about a battle in the adjacent kingdom in which one hundred soldiers had been engaged on either side, and all had died, each man in one army having chosen an opponent from the hostile army and having killed him, being himself killed by the other during the fray. This was too big a dose to be swallowed even by an Indian court. 'Really?' said the king. 'Your Majesty, I have uttered the simple truth. I saw the whole occurence with my own eyes,' said the noble. The king kept silent out of politeness, but characterised the story as 'passing strange'. He asked every one of his ministers and courtiers whether he believed that such an incident could have taken place. All, including Bhaskaracharya, professed unbelief in the story. Then the King asked Lilavathi whether she believed it to be true. 'I know it to be true,' said she, to the great wonder and joy of the noble, 'because I saw another strange event happen close to the place where the two hundred dead bodies lay. Two cobras of equal length, girth and strength began to swallow each other at the same time, each beginning with the other's tail, and finally swallowed each other and completely disappeared leaving no trace behind.' The king and the courtiers laughed loudly at this. The noble was furious and said, 'That tale about the cobras is a lie. How can two cobras of equal length, girth and strength swallow each other? At a certain point the swallowing must stop. Unless one was a bigger cobra, it could never have swallowed the other. In any case, both could not have disappeared. Matter is permanent. Whoever would believe such a silly story?' 'Those who believe your other silly story,' said Lilavathi, amidst roars of laughter.

A Suitable Punishment

Before leaving for court one morning, Akbar was playing with one of his grandsons. The mischievous child pointed at his grandfather's moustache.

'Oh look, Baba, there is something stuck on your moustache. Let me brush it off.'

Akbar bent down and the lad quickly plucked out a hair from the king's moustache.

'That hurt!' Akbar tried to catch the naughty fellow as he ran laughing out of reach.

Akbar was still thinking of this incident when he caught sight of Birbal in court that morning. He decided to trip his witty friend by asking him a trick question.

Akbar addressed all his nobles solemnly. 'This morning, some rascal plucked a hair from my moustache. What do you think would be a suitable punishment for such behaviour?'

The nobles were horrified to think that someone could do such a thing to the emperor. A chorus of responses arose.

'The culprit should be whipped fifty times!'

'Certainly, the death sentence for such a close attack on the king!'

'Each and every hair in his own moustache should be plucked out one by one as punishment.'

But Birbal said nothing. The emperor looked at him. 'Well, Birbal, what do you think would be a suitable punishment?'

'I think Your Majesty should catch the rascal, spank him and then give a big hug and a kiss.'

The nobles looked at Birbal in amazement.

'Now, why so lenient a punishment, Birbal? Do you think a person should be allowed to get away with an attack on the emperor's body?'

Birbal smiled. 'Only one of the emperor's own grandchildren would be able to get close enough to him to do such a thing. Only a little prince would have the impudence to pull a hair from his royal grandfather's moustache.

The emperor laughed. Birbal had seen through his trick question.

The King's Ambassador

Kings seldom called on each other in person because travel was tedious and dangerous. Instead, they sent important men in the kingdom as ambassadors to convey their messages. To show respect for each other, they would send lavish gifts.

Akbar sent Birbal on several diplomatic missions, especially to Hindu kings and chieftains. With his wit and charm, Birbal could accomplish what armies could not.

On one occasion, Birbal was sent to his former employer, the Raja of Rewa. Although the raja had accepted Akbar's superiority and had sent his son to the Mughal court, he had never come to pay his respects to the emperor in person. Akbar took this to be a sign of disobedience and was about to send an army against him, but was persuaded that the raja was just too timid to make the long journey on his own. Akbar sent Birbal to soothe the raja's fears and bring him into the court. The Raja brought magnificent rubies as a gift for the emperor. Birbal's diplomacy thus averted a war.

The Raja of Dungarpur (a Rajput kingdom) wanted Akbar to marry his daughter, but was hesitant to send her to the royal harem. Birbal was sent with another noble to Dungarpur. He calmed the raja's fears and escorted the princess safely to the emperor.

As it was well known that Birbal was close to the emperor, people would seek him out when they needed help at the court.

The Raja of Kajli, a kingdom in south India, sent an ambassador to Akbar with a special healing knife as a gift. For a long time the ambassador was unable to get an introduction to the emperor. Finally, he appealed to Birbal, who presented him to Akbar. The healing knife was duly received by the king. It is claimed that more than two hundred sick people were eventually cured by touching the knife. At another time, Bhupat Chohan, a rebel, came to Birbal in order to obtain forgiveness from the emperor. Birbal was also sent to appease Masum Khan Farankhudi who had rebelled against the emperor.

Birbal Travels to Burma

Hussain Khan was always fretting that he was not being treated fairly by the emperor. After all, his sister was married to Akbar. Shouldn't he have a more important position at court than that good-for-nothing commoner Birbal? Birbal was always travelling here and there as ambassador. Surely Hussain Khan could handle important diplomatic missions just as well, if not better. Once more, he had his sister appeal to the emperor on his behalf.

Akbar was weary of Hussain Khan's constant whining. It would be wonderful to get rid of him for some time. One morning, he summoned both Hussain Khan and Birbal to his presence. He gave them a sealed scroll. 'I want both of you to go to the kingdom of Burma and deliver my letter to the king personally. It is a very important matter. You must wait for his answer before you return.'

Hussain Khan was delighted to get something important to do at last. He was not so happy that he had to share the assignment with Birbal, but then it would be nice to have a companion on the long journey to Burma. He insisted that being the emperor's brother-in-law, he should be the one to make a formal speech and present Akbar's letter to the king of Burma. Birbal agreed. Both men set off the very next day with horses, servants and provisions for the trip.

Burma was a long way off, over a thousand miles away. It was a small but independent kingdom, and so far had had little to do with the Mughal emperor.

When Birbal and Hussain Khan finally arrived at the capital of Burma several weeks later, they went straight to the king's palace.

The king of Burma sat on his throne in a splendid palace, surrounded by his ministers and advisors. They were surprised when Akbar's emissaries were ushered in. What could the great emperor possibly want from them?

Hussain Khan's throat felt dry now that the time had come to make his speech. He hastily handed Akbar's letter to Birbal. Without hesitation, Birbal bowed to the king and made a long speech, full of courtly sentiments and lavish compliments. Hussain Khan couldn't help admiring how quickly Birbal was able to come up with the right things to say, even though he had not had time to prepare.

Birbal handed the sealed scroll over to the king. Both Birbal and Hussain Khan waited eagerly to learn what was in the letter. Birbal usually knew the contents of all the messages he carried for the emperor. This was the first time that he had travelled for so many weeks without knowing what it was.

The king's interpreter repeated the Persian contents of the letter in the Burmese language. Birbal and Hussain Khan could not understand a word he said. But they did notice the effect the letter had on the king and his nobles. They appeared to be utterly shocked and gaped at each other with open mouths.

Akbar's letter had requested that the king of Burma hang the two men who were the bearers of his message, on the night of the full moon. What a strange request! The Burmese peered closely at the two messengers from India. They did not seem to be wicked criminals. The king felt he had to have a meeting with his ministers before deciding what to do with the two strangers from India. Meanwhile, he ordered that the two men be removed from the court and kept under close guard. As soon as they were gone, the nobles clustered around the king.

'Why does Akbar want us to hang these poor fellows? They do not seem to be bad men,' one minister pondered.

'If they did something wrong, why did he not hang them himself?' asked another.

'Perhaps they are powerful men and Akbar is afraid to execute them in his own country,' suggested the chief minister.

'If they are powerful men, then surely it is not safe for us to kill them either. Their friends will come after us.'

'Emperor Akbar is a powerful man too. I cannot ignore this request he has sent all the way to me, or else he will be angry with me,' said the king.

The chief minister had an idea, 'Let me talk to the prisoners and try to learn from them why Emperor Akbar would wish to hang them. Perhaps that will help make things clear.'

Everyone agreed on the plan and the chief minister walked to the room where Birbal and Hussain Khan were kept under guard.

Meanwhile, the two ambassadors were wondering what was going on. Hussain Khan was becoming quite anxious. 'I do not know what was in that letter, Birbal, but it certainly made all of them very unhappy. What is going to become of us?'

'I don't know what will become of us,' said Birbal. 'But it does not look good. The king is treating us like prisoners instead of important guests.'

'I am the emperor's brother-in-law. They should not be treating me like this. I'm counting on you to get us out of this mess, whatever it is, Birbal. You are responsible for my safety. My sister will never forgive you if anyone should harm me.'

'Very well,' said Birbal. 'I will try to get us out of this mess. But you must agree with everything I say. Even repeat what I say, if necessary.'

Just then, the chief minister walked into the room. 'Emperor Akbar has asked us in his letter to hang both of you on the night of the full moon. Can you tell us why he would make such a strange request?'

Hussain Khan went pale and broke out in a sweat, but Birbal replied smoothly. 'But of course. You must follow Emperor Akbar's instructions exactly. Our king is a great and just man. He always has a good reason for everything he does.'

Hussain Khan managed to agree with Birbal as he had promised. 'Yes, yes. You must hang us on the night of the full moon, exactly as Emperor Akbar has ordered.'

The chief minister was even more mystified than before. The two men were actually quite eager to be hanged! And they refused to say 'why'.

He took this information back to the king's council. 'Well, let us go forward with Akbar's instructions,' the king decided. 'Perhaps these men will change their minds when they are faced with the gallows, and tell us what this is all about.'

Gallows were constructed in the palace courtyard, and on the night of the full moon Birbal and Hussain Khan were led to them. The king and his courtiers stood around watching.

In the meanwhile, Birbal had carefully tutored Hussain Khan about what he should say. As planned, Hussain Khan ran forward to the king of Burma. 'Your Majesty, I am Emperor Akbar's brother-in-law. I would like to be hanged first.'

'No, no, no!' Birbal protested. 'I was the one who handed you Emperor Akbar's letter, therefore I should be hanged first.'

The king and his ministers were utterly puzzled by this odd behaviour. The chief minister turned to Birbal. 'If you promise to tell us why you are so eager to be hanged, I will make sure you go first.'

'Very well, sire,' said Birbal, pretending to be greatly relieved, while Hussain Khan pouted and appeared to be angry. 'Astrologers have predicted that whoever is hanged first, on this night of the full moon, will become the king of Burma in the next life. Since Hussain Khan and I are closest to Emperor Akbar, he was hoping one of us would be the next king of Burma. This way he can make Burma a part of his empire without fighting a war.'

Aha! So this was Akbar's motive in having these men hanged here on the night of the full moon. No wonder they were eager to be hung first. The king was very concerned. He certainly did not want anyone but his son, the crown prince, to be the next king of Burma. And he never wanted Burma to be a part of Akbar's empire.

He ordered Birbal and Hussain Khan to be set free. The next morning they were carefully escorted out of the borders of the kingdom and sent on their way.

Several weeks later, Birbal and Hussain Khan arrived back at Akbar's court. The emperor greeted them warmly. He had been absolutely sure that Birbal would find a way to escape from the situation he had put them in. Hussain Khan had been taught a frightening lesson.

Akbar turned to his brother-in-law, 'Well, Hussain Khan, do you still wish to take Birbal's place as ambassador and counsellor?' Hussain Khan joined both palms and bowed low. 'Oh no, Your Majesty. Only Birbal can go on these dangerous missions. Only he has the wit and wisdom to handle these situations. I have no desire left to take his place.'

Who is the Real Shah?

The Shah of Persia had heard of Birbal and his cleverness in solving problems. He wanted to see this man in action, so he asked his cousin, the Emperor of Hindustan, to send Birbal to Persia for a visit. Akbar was only too happy to send Birbal to Persia, loaded with many fine gifts for the shah.

When Birbal arrived at the Persian capital, he was ushered into the shah's audience chamber. To his surprise, there were seven men, all dressed in rich robes and all seated on thrones. It was impossible to tell who the real shah was. All seven looked identical.

Birbal understood immediately that the shah wanted to test him to see if he could identify the real shah. Birbal looked carefully at the seven men. Then carefully and deliberately, he positioned himself in front of the man who was third from the left. He bowed deeply, touching his head with his right palm, which was the customary form of greeting, 'Your Majesty, the Emperor of Hindustan sends you his greetings and compliments. I have brought with me rich gifts as a token of his regard for you.'

The shah gasped in surprise. 'You are truly as clever as they say, Birbal. But tell me, how did you know that I was the real shah? You have never seen me before.'

'It was easy, Your Majesty. All the other men were looking at you, because you are their king. You alone had the assurance of authority. You looked straight at me.'

The shah was truly impressed with this demonstration of

Birbal's quick wits. He enjoyed his company and his humour
for several weeks before he sent him back to India, loaded with
presents for his cousin, Emperor Akbar.

The Friendship of Akbar and Birbal

The closeness between Akbar and Birbal was enhanced by the fact that the emperor saved his minister's life twice, once at considerable risk to his own safety.

The first time was in 1583, at a polo game that was being played during the celebrations of the Id festival. During the game, Birbal suddenly fell from his horse and became unconscious. It was Akbar who ran to his aid and revived him.

The following year, Akbar and his courtiers were observing an elephant fight at the polo ground. The emperor sat on a horse. In the middle of the fight, an elephant suddenly charged at Birbal. When he saw that his friend was in danger, Akbar urged his horse on and stood between the elephant and Birbal. As the angry elephant rushed at the emperor, the spectators cried out in fear for his life. But Akbar merely commanded the elephant to stop in an imperious manner. Recognising the voice of authority, the elephant suddenly stopped in its tracks.

Such a close friendship with the great emperor made several people envy Birbal. One such man was the scholar Badauni, who in the second part of his *Muntakhab-ut-Tawarikh* describes Akbar's court. Badauni was fanatical in his religious belief, and resented the influence of Abul Fazl and Birbal, who he believed had turned Akbar's mind away from Islam. He was shocked at Birbal for teaching the king strange Hindu ways like worshipping the sun. Badauni called Birbal 'accursed', 'wretch' and 'hellish dog'. He made many negative comments about Birbal's character. He even rejoiced when Birbal was killed in the battle against the Afghans. He blamed the defeat of the Mughal army on Birbal's wilfulness, stupidity and arrogance.

However, Badauni admitted that the emperor had never experienced such grief at the death of any Amir as he did at that of Birbal's. Even though he hated him so much, Badauni described Birhal as being 'possessed of a considerable amount of capacity and genius'. Coming from Badauni, this was high praise indeed.

Like many of Akbar's leading nobles, Birbal was not only a poet and orator; he was also a brave soldier who eventually commanded an army of 2,000 men. He died fighting in February 1586, during a battle against Afghans in Swat, a region on the north-west frontier of India, at the age of fifty-eight.

When the news of Birbal's death reached the emperor, Akbar was devastated. He did not eat for two days and nights. What upset him further was that Birbal's body had not been recovered. He could not even honour him in a state funeral that would show everyone how important he was to him. He missed his favourite companion greatly. It is said that losing Birbal was the greatest grief he had experienced since coming to the throne.

Chanakya and Firewood

Chanakya, the famous minister of Chandragupta, used to scrutinize even the expenditure of firewood in the emperor's kitchen. A certain quantity was weighed out and given, and if more was wanted, the minister's permission was necessary. One of the courtiers was disgusted at what he considered the mean conduct of the prime minister, and so went to Chanakya one day and told him that it was a great scandal that a great emperor like Chandragupta should have even his supply of firewood for the kitchen restricted.

'Wherein is Chandragupta a great emperor?' asked Chanakya.

'Because of his mighty empire from the Himalayas to the sea,' replied the courtier. 'How does His Imperial Majesty get his income?' asked Chankya.

'From his revenues,' replied the courtier.

'From whom are the revenues derived?' asked the prime minister.

'From the ryots,' replied the courtier.

'Will a ryot waste firewood?' asked Chanakya.

'Of course, not,' said the courtier. 'The wretched fellow will go a mile to pick up a dry twig, and will save even the charcoal for further use.'

'When that is so,' said Chanakya, 'how can His Imperial Majesty, who is but the trustee of the revenues derived from such ryots, be allowed to waste firewood?' Th courtier retired in confusion.

Birbal and the Mad Elephant

Akbar liked taking chances and doing dangerous things. Once, as a young man, he had mounted one of the most violent elephants in the stable and had gone in chase of another elephant. People in the court were aghast because they were sure the emperor would be killed. Instead, Akbar enjoyed the episode very much.

Birbal was a brave man too, but he was far more cautious than his master. 'Why court danger if you can avoid it?' was his belief.

Akbar liked to tease Birbal by putting him in situations where he would have to confront danger. As Birbal had always scolded the king about the dangers of riding violent elephants, Akbar thought he would play a trick on him.

One day, when Birbal was walking towards the palace through a narrow lane, Akbar had one of the most dangerous elephants in the stables let loose. He watched from the balcony to see what Birbal would do. Had Akbar been in his shoes, he probably would have found a way to confront the angry beast and climb on to its back. That is how he did things. He was the king; he had to master every situation.

Birbal believed in using his mind rather than physical power. When he saw the enraged elephant come charging down the narrow lane towards him, he realised he was trapped. If he were to turn around and run back, the elephant would have chased him down and trampled him to death. Suddenly he spotted a stray dog. Swiftly, he lifted up the animal and flung it at the elephant.

Confused by the dog's barks and yelps, the elephant stopped in his tracks. Birbal took advantage of the elephant's hesitation and escaped from the lane.

Akbar clapped his hands. Even though he would have handled the situation differently, he couldn't help admiring Birbal's presence of mind.

Breadth or Depth

A Hindu king, anxious to advance education in his country, was torn between the claims of elementary education for the masses and advanced education for the few. To resolve his doubt, he went to a holy man living in the vicinity and consulted him. 'Have both,' was the reply. 'Depth and breadth are both to be desired. Universal elementary education will, in addition to making all people literate, reveal those fit for higher education, while the latter will, in addition to advancing knowledge, make the former more efficient.' 'But, unfortunately, I have not enough money for both,' said the king. 'So I have to choose between the two alternatives. Some of my advisers want me to choose the advanced education for the few, saying that the literacy of the masses can wait and that its virtues are exaggerated, pointing out that Akbar, though illiterate, was greater than any educated man now.' 'Did they think of Asoka, the literate, how his very words come to us across the centuries, through his written edicts, and how Akbar, because of his illiteracy, has failed to speak to us in his own words? They very words of a great saint are far more precious than the best summaries by others, and only literacy can ensure such life after death to our words. So, the best course is what I have indicated above,' replied the holy man. 'That not being possible, the next best is to give elementary education for all, postponing the advanced education till you get funds.

The alternative you mentioned is the worst. Which is better, big lights in the palace and a few selected houses, and no lights at all in the smaller ones, or, small lights in every house including the palace?'

The Crows of Agra

Every time the emperor wished to know something, he turned to Birbal. 'Birbal, what…?,' 'Birbal, why…?,' 'Birbal how…?,' he always seemed to be asking, as though Birbal knew everything. This made some of the other nobles in court jealous.

A small group of learned men decided to bring the matter up in court. 'Your Majesty, you consult Birbal for solutions to every problem, as though he is the only man in court with any brains. We are also quite intelligent. Sometimes you should give us the opportunity to serve you.'

'Very well, then,' said the emperor immediately. Some of the scholars in court took themselves so seriously. He loved to poke fun at them. 'Tell me, how many crows are there in the city of Agra?'

The nobles rolled their eyes in astonishment. What sort of a question was this? Agra was full of crows. Thousands of them. Always cawing and making pests of themselves.

'Surely you jest, Your Majesty. Only Allah would know the answer to this question!' one courtier said, throwing up his hands.

Stroking his beard, another man answered thoughtfully: 'To take a census of the crows, I would need two hundred men or so, Your Majesty. It would take us about a year to get you an accurate count of all the crows in the city.' He saw an opportunity for himself as perhaps the Head of the Bureau of Crow Counting.

'But crows don't sit still to be counted, Your Majesty'

protested a third noble. 'No one can ever claim to get an accurate count of the crows in the city.'

Akbar turned to Birbal who was standing beside him, shielding his smile with his hand. He could see that the king was just having fun at the expense of the discontented nobles. 'Well, Birbal, what do you say? How many crows are there in the city of Agra?'

Without a moment's hesitation, Birbal replied, 'Thirty thousand, four hundred and eighty-three, Your Majesty.'

Immediately, one of the nobles pounced on him. 'It is easy enough to come up with a number. But how do we know it is true? What if we were to actually count the crows and there were less than you say?'

Completely unruffled, Birbal responded quickly. 'Ah, that would only mean that several of the crows of Agra are in other cities visiting their friends and relatives.'

Akbar was thoroughly enjoying the discussion. He loved to see how smoothly Birbal could handle the trickiest of problems.

Unwilling to let go of the argument, the noble persisted, 'But what if there are more crows than thirty thousand, four hundred and eighty-three, Birbal?'

'But of course, they would be the crows from other cities visiting their friends and relatives in Agra.'

Akbar burst out laughing and clapped his hands. Nobody could challenge Birbal's answer. The emperor turned to the downcast nobles. 'Now do you see why I turn to Birbal for everything? He always has the answer.'

Birbal bowed low. But the nobles continued to mutter and grumble about the attention he received from the king.

The Three Sanyasis

A king of old sent an ambassador with three sanyasis to a neighbouring king, asking him to pick out the best, the next best, and the worst in half an hour. The king, to whom these holy men were sent, adopted a simple device. He called the first sanyasi in, seated him on a gold throne by his side and talked to him for five minutes. Then he sent him away and called the second, seated him on a silver throne and talked with him for five minutes. After that, he sent him away and called the third, seated him on a copper throne and talked with him for five minutes. Then he sent him away also. Five minutes later, the king went with the ambassador to the three sanyasis. He called the first aside and asked him, 'Of what material was the throne on which you sat made?'

'I don't know,' replied he.

'Do you know on what thrones your two comrades sat?' asked the king.

'I do not,' replied the first sanyasi.

The king then called the second sanyasi aside and asked him, 'Of what material was the throne on which you sat made?'

'It was made of silver,' replied he. 'And those on which your two comrades sat?' asked the king.

'I did not enquire,' replied the sanyasi. The king then called the third sanyasi aside and asked him, 'Of what material was the throne on which you sat made?'

'Of copper,' replied the sanyasi.

'And those on which your two comrades sat?' enquired the
king. 'My brother there,' replied the third sanyasi, pointing to
the second 'sat on a silver throne. I ascertained it from him. As
for the first sanyasi, I didn't ask him, since he was plunged in
his own meditation.'

The king told the ambassador, who too had heard all this,
'The first sanyasi is the best, the second the next best, and the
third the worst. The first was so intent upon God that he never
noted the shining gold on which he was sitting, much less did
he ask the others on what thrones they sat. The second was
worldly enough to note the material of the throne on which he
sat, though he was not vulgar enough to ask his companions on
what thrones they sat. The third not only noted the material of
the throne on which he himself sat, but was also vulgar enough
to enquire of the second on what throne he sat.'

The King Admires Birbal

Yusuf Khan was envious of Birbal. He seemed so clever and sure of himself. Akbar made it quite obvious that he thought very highly of him. He sent him on important missions and gave him special favours and honours. The emperor seemed to think that Birbal could do no wrong. Wouldn't it be nice if once, just once, Birbal could be made to look foolish in the eyes of the emperor?

Yusuf Khan became quite obsessed with the idea of discrediting Birbal. He waited for a time when Birbal was away from court and then approached Akbar.

'Your Majesty I have heard Birbal boast that he can read men's minds. No doubt he is a wonderfully clever man. No ordinary human could do such a thing.'

Yusuf Khan's friend, who was part of the scheme, said, 'But everyone knows that Birbal is the cleverest man in the kingdom. Why, reading men's thoughts should be no problem for a genius like him!'

Both men knew that although the emperor loved Birbal, he did get quite irritated when a man other than himself was praised so highly.

And sure enough, Akbar snorted. 'So, Birbal claims he can read men's thoughts, does he? It would be nice then, to watch a demonstration of his so-called powers.'

When Birbal returned to court, Yusuf Khan and his friend waited eagerly for the emperor to bring up the subject. At the end of the morning, after Akbar had finished congratulating

Birbal on the mission he had just handled so successfully, he commented. 'You are indeed a very clever man, Birbal. I have heard that you claim to be able to read men's minds.'

Birbal had sensed that something was afoot when he had entered the court that morning. Yusuf Khan and his friend were whispering to each other and looking at him in a malicious way. Now, when he glanced in their direction, they were sitting upright, smiling expectantly. He guessed that this was their idea. They were waiting to see him fail in front of the emperor.

Unperturbed, Birbal bowed low. 'Your Majesty honours me too much. How could one as humble and lowly as myself ever read the lofty thoughts of the King of Kings?'

Then he straightened up and looked around. 'But I can say with confidence that I can read the minds of every one of the men gathered in this room. There is only one thought in all their loyal minds: they pray to the Almighty to bless you with a long and healthy life so that you can rule over us forever.' He turned to Yusuf Khan. 'Well, my dear Yusuf Khan, have I read your mind correctly or do you disagree with me?'

Birbal knew full well that Yusuf Khan would never dare to deny that he was thinking of anything but the king's welfare. None of the nobles in the room had the courage to challenge Birbal's statement. Naturally, they did not wish the king to think they were disloyal. They would have to agree that Birbal had read their minds correctly. One and all murmured their assent. Yusuf Khan squirmed in his chair. Quick-thinking Birbal had avoided the trap that had been so carefully set for him. In fact, he managed to impress Akbar even more with his diplomatic handling of the situation.

Akbar smiled broadly. He realised now what Yusuf Khan had been trying to do and was delighted to see Birbal put him in his place.

Must Be in Bed for Seven Days

A king of old wanted to pass a law that any poor man who was in bed for more than seven days would be regarded as very sick, and given free meals by the state. His minister became seriously alarmed, and said to the king, 'Sire, all the beggars and idlers will soon lie in bed for seven days, pretending to be sick, and impoverish our State by getting free food from it.'

'Those people will never accept my condition,' said the king. 'Bring the cleverest scoundrel among the idlers and beggars in our land, and I shall prove to you that you are wrong.'

The minister brought the most idle beggar in the whole land and told him that he would receive free food, if he lay in bed for seven days continuously. 'What good luck!' said the beggar, 'I need no longer wander in search of food.'

'Mind you,' said the king, 'you must not stir out of your bed. Every one of your wants will be attended to by others.'

'What unheard of good luck!' exclaimed the beggar, and his face beamed with joy.

'Sire,' said the minister, 'my prediction is borne out.'

'Wait till the experiment has finished,' replied the king.

So the beggar was put to bed, and an attendant was provided to look after his wants, and see that he did not get out of the bed. For the first day, the beggar was most joyous and never left the bed or wanted to leave it. The luxury of such a rest, with such attendance, acted as an intoxicant on him. The next day, the sweetness lessened just a bit, but was still sufficiently strong. The day after that the beggar's legs began to itch for a short walk. The beggar wanted to rise up from his bed, but was prevented by the attendant, who warned him about the *sine qua non* for getting free food. On the fourth day, the beggar prayed hard to be allowed just to go to the window for a few minutes, but to no purpose. Then, he again made a supreme effort and lay down for an hour or two without stirring. But all to no purpose. In the evening the beggar told the attendant that he wanted no free meals, if they were to be purchased at the cost of not stirring out of the bed for three more days. 'Good Heavens!' said the beggar, 'I can get free meals elsewhere and stay at perfect liberty to wander about. Those meals taste better than these which I get here, because I would also be more hungry. What appeared to be a light condition, I find to be the most difficult imaginable. Give me back my liberty, and I renounce all right to free meals from the State.' Saying this, the beggar took his stick from the corner and rushed out before the attendant knew what was happening.

Birbal Goes to Heaven

Some courtiers could not get over their hatred for Birbal. They blamed their lack of success in court not on their lack of abilities, but on Birbal. If Birbal were not around, perhaps they would get promoted.

A few of them hated him so passionately that they plotted to kill him. They took Akbar's barber into confidence. Since he shaved the king every day, he had an opportunity to speak privately to the king without Birbal around. They gave the barber a bag of gold coins and promised him more if their plot succeeded. The greedy barber thought this was an easy way to make some money.

The next day, when shaving Akbar, he said, 'Your Majesty have you ever thought of what life must be like in the next world? For example, wouldn't it be nice to know how your father, His Majesty, Emperor Humayun, God rest his soul, is doing in the other world? I often wonder if he is happy and if he needs anything.'

'Yes, it would be nice to know,' Akbar admitted. 'But I have no means of finding out.'

'Perhaps I can help you here, Your Majesty,' the barber suggested eagerly. 'I recently met a holy man who can send people to the other world.'

'Hah! That is easy enough to do!' the emperor snorted. 'All I have to do is to execute someone to send him to the other world.'

'But this holy man gave me a mantra that can bring them

back, sire!' the barber exclaimed. 'I saw with my own eyes. He piled a thousand bales of hay on an open field. Then he burned a man alive on this huge pyre. All the man had to do was to chant the mantra just before the fire was lit. Later, the man returned from the other world and told everyone how he had met his departed relatives there.

'It sounds perfectly simple, but whom should we send? Would you like to go?' offered the emperor, wondering where this strange story would lead to.

'Oh no, not me!' the barber replied immediately, breaking out into a sweat. 'I am not important enough to go to heaven, sire. Your ancestors would be most insulted if a most humble and miserable speck of dust like myself were to inquire after them! It should be someone really important, Your Majesty. Someone you trust completely. Someone wise and clever who can conduct himself in any situation. For example, a man such as Raja Birbal. A perfect choice!'

'Aha!' thought Akbar, when he heard Birbal's name. 'So this is yet another plot to get rid of Birbal. Let me play along with this foolish man and see what happens. Birbal will teach him a lesson.' He was completely confident that Birbal would find a way out of the predicament. He always did.

At court that day, the emperor summoned Birbal and informed him that he had decided to send him as an ambassador to heaven to inquire after his dead father's health and comfort. The wicked nobles who had plotted Birbal's downfall rubbed their hands in glee to see their plans succeeding.

'It will be my greatest honour, Jahanpanah! My life and everything I own are at your disposal,' said Birbal bowing low. He immediately realised that this was the work of his enemies. He knew he had lots of them at court. 'But please, Your Majesty, may I have a month to prepare for this journey? Who knows if and when I will return?'

'Gladly!' said the emperor. 'You may have as much time as you want.'

Birbal hired some trusted workmen to build a secret tunnel from the open field outside the city to his home. When it was ready, he had a thousand bundles of hay piled right next to the hidden opening of the secret tunnel.

On the appointed day, Akbar, his nobles, indeed the entire town turned out to see Birbal embark on this strange journey to heaven. Birbal sat atop the bundles of hay and chanted the mantra that the barber had given him. Then, saluting the emperor, he gave the order to light the pyre. Amid the flames, smoke, noise and confusion, Birbal escaped through the door of the secret tunnel.

Birbal remained in hiding for several months. The wicked nobles were delighted. It seemed that at long last they had succeeded in getting rid of Akbar's favourite.

Akbar, meanwhile, was getting sadder and sadder without Birbal's cheerful company. Surely, Birbal had found a way to escape from the fire. But where on earth was he?

Then one day, Birbal reappeared at court. No one recognized him. His hair was shaggy and unkempt, and he had grown a long beard. He bowed low at Akbar's feet. Of course, Akbar was overjoyed to see him again.

'Jahanpanah, I am back from heaven. I met His Majesty, the Emperor Humayun, your dear departed father, God rest his soul, and he sends you his love.'

'Well, how is my dear father?' said Akbar, playing along with Birbal for the benefit of the court. The wicked nobles sat astounded to see their rival, safe and sound, returned from the dead.

'He is very happy and content,' said Birbal. 'Except for one thing. There are no barbers in heaven. You see how shaggy and unkempt my hair has become in just a few weeks. You can imagine what your father looks like!'

'I know just the man to do the job,'Akbar chuckled delightedly. Birbal had found the perfect way to pay back his enemies. He summoned the greedy barber to the court and informed him that he was sending him to heaven to cut his father's hair.

'Prepare to ascend the pyre tomorrow,' he ordered.

The barber took to his heels and was never seen again!

Krishna Deva Raya and the Minister's Advice

Krishna Deva Raya, the celebrated Emperor of Vijayanagar, was almost continuously engaged in bitter wars with the Muhammadan Sultans of the Deccan. One day, a minister said to him, 'Oh, great king, I have always admired your wisdom, but one thing puzzles me. You are forever fighting against our enemies the Muhammadans, but still you allow many Muhammadans to live and prosper in your dominions and even in the capital city; you give Muhammadans responsible posts; you even enlist them in your army and contribute heavy sums towards the services in the mosque, constructed in the centre of this city at great expense to the State. This is very strange. The proper thing would be to pull down this mosque and massacre or at least exile all the Muhammadans in your vast dominions.'

The great king smiled and said:

'Simply because an enemy's horse bites you, are you therefore to kill your own faithful horses for their mere sin in belonging to the same race? By killing or oppressing my faithful Muhammadan subjects, I would be only showing myself unworthy to be a king, who ought to be scrupulously just in his actions. Again, if I pull down the mosque and kill the Muhammadans for the crime of their belonging to a particular religion, I shall create distrust even among the Hindus, who will think that if I should, by any chance, become a convert to another religion, I shall merecilessly kill them and pull down their temples regardless of justice. A king should do nothing which is not just.'

Harishchandra—the Truthful King

Harishchandra, the son of Trishanku, was an ancestor of Rama. He ruled over Ayodhya with his wife Taramati and son Rohitashwa. He was a just and kind king. He learnt the value of truth. He gained fame for his truthfulness, honesty and integrity. This fame got to the gods in heaven, and they decided to test him. The sage Vishwamitra was selected to be the one to test the king. Vishwamitra tried many things to get Harishchandra to lie; all his efforts proved in vain. Harishchandra was as committed to his values as had been heard by the gods.

Finally, Vishwamitra manipulated circumstances into a situation where Harishchandra was obliged to give up his kingdom and all his possessions to the sage. Harishchandra gave up his kingdom with a smile, and with his wife and son, wearing only rags and barks of trees, set out for the forest. Stunned by such generosity, and in a last attempt at provoking the king, Vishwamitra asked him for the *Dakshina*.

The king, having given up everything he owned, had nothing left to give as *Dakshina*. Vishwamitra gave him the grace period of a month to pay the *Dakshina*.

Harishchandra wandered all over the country, trying to earn enough money to pay the sage, but even the gods seemed to be against him, for he was unsuccessful wherever he went. Finally, he reached the holy city of Kashi—today known as Varanasi. Even in this crowded city, Harishchandra was unable to find any employment.

The grace period was drawing to a close, and Harishchandra was worried. Finally his wife, Taramati, who was as righteous as her husband, made a suggestion, 'I have a suggestion to make, which, though it sounds improper, is the only way left to us. There is a great demand in this city for slaves, who can work for the many rich people who live here. Please sell me and use the money to pay off the sage. Later, when you make enough money, you can buy me back again.' Harishchandra was aghast at this suggestion! 'Sell off my wife, who has stood by me through all my troubles! Impossible!' he cried. However, as time passed, and he was unable to earn money, he had to give in to his wife and agreed to sell her. Taking his wife to the slave market, he sold her to the highest bidder, an aged Brahmin who agreed to pay even more for the little boy accompanying her. Faced with no choice, Harishchandra accepted the money and let his wife and child go with the Brahmin. Just then, Vishwamitra arrived and demanded his *Dakshina* again, and Harishchandra handed over all the money he had just received, but Vishwamitra was not satisfied. He said, 'Is this the *Dakshina* you pay a sage of my calibre? I cannot accept such a pittance!' As Harishchandra was pondering over what to do, a *chandala*—a man of the lowest of the lower castes, those who are only permitted to work and live on cremation grounds—arrived, and said he was looking for an able bodied man to work for him. Immediately Vishwamitra turned to Harishchandra and said, 'Why don't you sell yourself to this man and pay me my due?'

Harishchandra was appalled! Chandalas were considered untouchables! When it was forbidden to even touch a *chandala*, he, a king, had to work for a *chandala*! How had he fallen to such a low state, lower than even a *chandala*! Vishwamitra was finally satisfied with the money he received, and left, leaving Harishchandra with the *chandala*. The *chandala* put Harishchandra to work in the cremation ground. He was continually troubled by thoughts of his wife and son. Time passed, and Harishchandra grew used to the work. His wife and son too got used to the poverty and the hard life they led, working in the Brahmin's house. One day, the young boy went to the garden to collect flowers, was bitten by a snake, and died. Taramati was disconsolate! She cried and cried, but finally she had to agree to consign the body to flames, and started for the cremation ground with her child in her arms. Harishchandra was on duty at the cremation ground, and he saw the woman bring a child for cremation. Poverty and difficulty had so changed all of them so much, that neither of them recognized the other. As per his duty, Harishchandra asked for the charge of cremation. Taramati began crying, saying, 'I am a slave and have nothing except these clothes on my body. Even my only child is dead! What can I pay you?' Harishchandra was moved by her piteous cry, but he could not budge from his duty of collecting the charge. Suddenly he noticed that the woman was wearing a 'mangalsutra'—the sign of her marriage—and said, 'Woman, why do you lie when you say you have nothing to give? You can give me your mangalsutra in exchange for the cremation!' Taramati was astonished! Her mangalsutra was a special one which could only be seen by her husband! She burst into tears at her predicament, and said, 'My Lord, we must have committed many sins in our previous lives to be in this state today. I am your wife, but you do not recognize me! This is our son, who is a prince, but lies here, dead, without even the benefit of cremation!' When his wife spoke thus, Harishchandra recognized her, and wept for his dear son, as well as their condition, but would not budge. 'It is my duty to collect this tax, and I shall never budge from my duty, no matter what happens!' he said. Taramati was as good and virtuous as her husband, and she said, 'All I have are the clothes on my body. Will you accept half of them and cremate our child?' When Harishchandra agreed, she started tearing off her clothes, but just then, the heavens erupted in applause! The gods in heaven rained flowers on the couple, and Vishwamitra appeared. He said, 'O King, all the troubles you have faced have been created by the gods to test your commitment to truth and honesty. You have not only emerged unscathed from these tests, but have earned a place in heaven due to your merits.' As the sage said these words, the little boy lying dead on the pyre sat up and rubbed his eyes, as if waking from sleep. Harishchandra was thrilled to see his son alive, and glad to hear that his troubles were ending.